# ROMANS

## Chapters 1—8

## J. Vernon McGee

THOMAS NELSON PUBLISHERS

*Nashville • Atlanta • London • Vancouver*

Published in Nashville, Tennessee, by Thomas Nelson, Inc.

Scripture quotations are from the KING JAMES VERSION of the Bible.

### Library of Congress Cataloging-in-Publication Data

McGee, J. Vernon (John Vernon), 1904–1988
    [Thru the Bible with J. Vernon McGee]
    Thru the Bible commentary series / J. Vernon McGee.
      p.    cm.
    Reprint. Originally published: Thru the Bible with J. Vernon
McGee. 1975.
    Includes bibliographical references.
    ISBN 0-7852-1046-6 (TR)
    ISBN 0-7852-1105-5 (NRM)
    1. Bible—Commentaries.  I. Title.
BS491.2.M37  1991
220.7′7—dc20                         90–41340
                                         CIP

Printed in the United States of America

3 4 5 6 7 8 9 — 99 98 97 96

# CONTENTS

## ROMANS—Chapters 1—8

# PREFACE

The radio broadcasts of the Thru the Bible Radio five-year program were transcribed, edited, and published first in single-volume paperbacks to accommodate the radio audience.

There has been a minimal amount of further editing for this publication. Therefore, these messages are not the word-for-word recording of the taped messages which went out over the air. The changes were necessary to accommodate a reading audience rather than a listening audience.

These are popular messages, prepared originally for a radio audience. They should not be considered a commentary on the entire Bible in any sense of that term. These messages are devoid of any attempt to present a theological or technical commentary on the Bible. Behind these messages is a great deal of research and study in order to interpret the Bible from a popular rather than from a scholarly (and too-often boring) viewpoint.

We have definitely and deliberately attempted "to put the cookies on the bottom shelf so that the kiddies could get them."

The fact that these messages have been translated into many languages for radio broadcasting and have been received with enthusiasm reveals the need for a simple teaching of the whole Bible for the masses of the world.

I am indebted to many people and to many sources for bringing this volume into existence. I should express my especial thanks to my secretary, Gertrude Cutler, who supervised the editorial work; to Dr. Elliott R. Cole, my associate, who handled all the detailed work with the publishers; and finally, to my wife Ruth for tenaciously encouraging me from the beginning to put my notes and messages into printed form.

Solomon wrote, ". . . of making many books there is no end; and much study is a weariness of the flesh" (Eccl. 12:12). On a sea of books that flood the marketplace, we launch this series of THRU THE BIBLE with the hope that it might draw many to the one Book, *The Bible*.

J. VERNON McGEE

# The Epistle to the
# ROMANS

## INTRODUCTION

Let me say just a word concerning Paul the apostle. With his writings we actually come now to a different method of revelation. God has used many ways to communicate to man. He gave the Pentateuch—the Law—through Moses. He gave history, He gave poetry, and He gave prophecy. He gave the Gospels, and now we come to a new section: the Epistles, the majority of which were written by Paul.

Adolf Deissmann tried to make a distinction between epistles and letters. Having examined the papyri that were found at Oxyrhynchus in Egypt, he made a decision between literary and nonliterary documents, placing the epistles of Paul in the latter category, thereby making them letters rather than epistles. However, a great many scholars today think this is an entirely false division.

These letters that we have—these epistles—are so warm and so personal that, as far as you and I are concerned, it is just as if they came by special delivery mail to us today. The Lord is speaking to us personally in each one of these very wonderful letters that Paul and the other apostles wrote to the churches. Nevertheless, Romans contains the great gospel manifesto for the world. To Paul the gospel was the great ecumenical movement and Rome was the center of that world for which Christ died. Paul's Epistle to the Romans is both an epistle and a letter.

Paul made this statement in Romans 15:15–16, "Nevertheless, brethren, I have written the more boldly unto you in some sort, as putting you in mind, because of the grace that is given to me of God, that I should be the minister of Jesus Christ to the Gentiles, ministering the gospel of God, that the offering up of the Gentiles might be acceptable, being sanctified by the Holy Ghost." Paul made it very clear here that he was the apostle to the Gentiles. He also made it clear that Simon Peter was the apostle to the nation Israel. For instance, in Galatians he said, "(For he that wrought effectually in Peter to the apostleship of the circumcision, the same was mighty in me toward the Gentiles:) and when James, Cephas, and John, who seemed to be pillars, perceived the grace that was given unto me, they gave to me and Barnabas the right hands of fellowship; that we should go unto the heathen, and they unto the circumcision" (Gal. 2:8–9). Therefore you see that Paul was peculiarly the apostle to the Gentiles. When you read the last chapter of Romans and see all those people that Paul knew, you will find that most of them were Gentiles. The church in Rome was largely a gentile church.

Paul also made the point that, if somebody else had founded the church in Rome, he would never have gone there. Instead, he said that he was eager to go there. "So as much as in me is, I am ready to preach the Gospel to you that are at Rome also" (Rom. 1:15). He wanted to go to Rome to preach the gospel. In Acts 26 Paul recounted to Agrippa the message the Lord gave to him when He appeared to him: "Delivering thee from the people, and from the Gentiles, unto whom now I send thee, to open their eyes, and turn them from darkness to light, and from the power of Satan unto God, that they may receive forgiveness of sins, and inheritance among them which are sanctified by faith that is in me" (Acts 26:17–18).

Further, Paul would never have gone to Rome, although he was eager to go, if anyone else had preached the gospel there ahead of him. In Romans 15:20 he said, "Yea, so have I strived to preach the gospel, not where Christ was named, lest I should build upon another man's foundation." Paul, my friend, just didn't go where another apostle had been. We can conclude, therefore, that no other apostle had been to Rome.

Now that leads me to say a word about Rome, and the question is: Who founded the church in Rome? I am going to make a rather unusual statement here: Paul is the one who founded the church in

Rome, and he founded it, as it were, by "long distance" and used the "remote control" of an apostle to write and guide its course.

Let me make this very clear. You see, Rome was a tremendous city. Paul had never been there, no other apostle had been there, and yet a church came into existence. How did it come into existence? Well, Paul, as he moved throughout the Roman Empire, won men and women to Christ. Rome had a strong drawing power, and many people were in Rome who had met Paul throughout the Roman Empire. You might ask, "Do you know that?" Oh, yes, we have a very striking example of that in Acts where we find Paul going to Corinth. "After these things Paul departed from Athens, and came to Corinth; and found a certain Jew named Aquila, born in Pontus, lately come from Italy, with his wife Priscilla; (because that Claudius had commanded all Jews to depart from Rome:) and came unto them. And because he was of the same craft, he abode with them, and wrought: for by their occupation they were tentmakers" (Acts 18:1–3). Paul had met Aquila and Priscilla—their home was in Rome, but there had been a wave of anti-Semitism; Claudius the emperor had persecuted them, and this couple had left Rome. They went to Corinth. We find later that they went with Paul to Ephesus and became real witnesses for Christ. Then, when Paul wrote the Epistle to the Romans, they had returned to Rome, and Paul sent greetings to them. We do have this very personal word in Acts concerning this couple. What about the others? Well, Paul did know them. That means he had also met them somewhere and had led them to Christ. Paul was the founder of the church at Rome by "long distance"—by leading folk to Christ who later gravitated to Rome.

Paul knew Rome although he had not been inside her city limits at the time of the writing of the Roman epistle. Rome was like a great ship passing in the night, casting up waves that broke on distant shores. Her influence was like a radio broadcast, penetrating every corner and crevice of the empire. Paul had visited Roman colonies such as Philippi and Thessalonica, and there he had seen Roman customs, laws, languages, styles, and culture on exhibit. He had walked on Roman roads, had met Roman soldiers on the highways and in the marketplaces, and he had slept in Roman jails. Paul had appeared before Roman magistrates, and he had enjoyed the benefits of Roman citizenship. You see, Paul knew all about Rome although he was yet to visit there. From the vantage point of the world's capital, he was to preach the global gospel to a lost world that God loved so much that He gave His Son to die, that whosoever believed on Him might not perish but have eternal life.

Rome was like a great magnet: It drew men and women from the ends of the then-known world to its center. As Paul and the other apostles crisscrossed in the hinterland of this colossal empire, they brought multitudes to the foot of the Cross. Churches were established in most of the great cities of this empire. In the course of time, many Christians were drawn to the center of this great juggernaut. The saying that "all roads lead to Rome" was more than just a bromide. As Christians congregated in this great metropolis, a visible church came into existence. Probably no individual man established the church in Rome. Converts of Paul and the other apostles from the fringe of the empire went to Rome, and a local church was established by them. Certainly, Peter did not establish the church or have anything to do with it, as his sermon on Pentecost and following sermons were directed to Israelites only. Not until the conversion of Cornelius was Peter convinced that Gentiles were included in the body of believers.

Summarizing, we have found that Paul is the one writing to the Romans. He was to visit Rome later, although he knew it very well already. And Paul was the founder of the church in Rome.

As we approach this great epistle, I feel totally inadequate because of its great theme, which is the righteousness of God. It is a message that I have attempted over the years to proclaim. And it is the message, by the way, that the world today as a whole does not want to hear, nor does it want to accept it. The world likes to hear, friend, about the glory of mankind. It likes to have mankind rather than God exalted. Now I am convinced in my own mind that any ministry today that attempts to teach the glory of man—which does not present the total depravity of the human family and does not reveal that man is totally corrupt and is a ruined creature, any teaching that does not deal with this great truth—will not lift mankind, nor will it offer a remedy. The only remedy for man's sin is the perfect remedy that we have in Christ, that which God has provided for a lost race. This is the great message of Romans.

Friend, may I say to you that the thief on the cross had been declared unfit to live in the Roman Empire and was being executed. But the Lord Jesus said that He was going to make him fit for heaven and told him, ". . . Today shalt thou be with me in paradise" (Luke 23:43). God takes lost sinners—like I am, like you are—and He brings them into the family of God and makes them sons of God. And He does it because of Christ's death upon the Cross—not because there is any merit in us whatsoever. This is the great message of Romans.

It was Godet, the Swiss commentator, who said that the Reformation was certainly the work of the Epistle to the Romans (and that of Galatians also) and that it is probable that every great spiritual renovation in the church will always be linked both in cause and in effect to a deeper knowledge of this book. It was Martin Luther who wrote that the Epistle to the Romans is "the true masterpiece of the New Testament and the very purest Gospel, which is well worthy and deserving that a Christian man should not only learn it by heart, word for word, but also that he should daily deal with it as the daily bread of men's souls. It can never be too much or too well read or studied; and the more it is handled, the more precious it becomes, and the better it tastes."

Chrysostom, one of the early church fathers, had the epistle read to him twice a week. And it was Coleridge who said that the Epistle to the Romans was the most profound writing that exists. Further, we find that one of the great scientists turned to this book, and he found that it gave a real faith. This man, Michael Faraday, was asked on his deathbed by a reporter, "What are your speculations now?" Faraday said, "I have no speculations. My faith is firmly fixed in Christ my Savior who died for me, and who has made a way for me to go to heaven."

May I say to you, this is the epistle that transformed that Bedford tinker by the name of John Bunyan. A few years ago I walked through the cemetery where he is buried, and I thought of what that man had done and said. You know, he was no intellectual giant, nor was he a poet, but he wrote a book that has been exceeded in sales by only one other, the Bible. That book is Bunyan's *Pilgrim's Progress*. It is a story of a sinner saved by grace, and that sinner was John Bunyan. And the record of history is that this man read and studied the Epistle to the Romans, and he told its profound story in his own life's story, the story of Pilgrim—that he came to the Cross, that the burden of sin rolled off, and that he began that journey to the Celestial City.

Let me urge you to do something that will pay you amazing dividends: read the Book of Romans, and read it regularly. This epistle requires all the mental make-up we have, and in addition, it must be bathed in prayer and supplication so that the Holy Spirit can teach us. Yet every Christian should make an effort to know Romans, for this book will ground the believer in the faith.

# OUTLINE

I. **Doctrinal, Chapters 1—8**
   *("Faith")*
   A. Justification of the Sinner, Chapters 1:1—5:11
      1. Introduction, Chapter 1:1–17
         (a) Paul's Personal Greeting, Chapter 1:1–7
         (b) Paul's Personal Purpose, Chapter 1:8–13
         (c) Paul's Three "I Am's," Chapter 1:14–17
             *(Key verses, 16–17—the revelation of the righteousness of God)*
      2. Revelation of the Sin of Man, Chapters 1:18—3:20
         *(This is "Sinnerama." Universal fact: Man is a sinner. Ecumenical movement is away from God. Axiom: World is guilty before God—all need righteousness.)*
         (a) Revelation of the Wrath of God Against Sin of Man, Chapter 1:18–32
             (1) Natural Revelation of God (Original Version), Chapter 1:18–20
             (2) Subnatural Response of Man (Revision), Chapter 1:21–23
             (3) Unnatural Retrogression of Man (Perversion), Chapter 1:24–27
             (4) Supernatural Requittal of God (Inversion), Chapter 1:28–32
         (b) Revelation of the Sin of Good People, Chapter 2:1–16
             *(Respectable people need righteousness.)*
         (c) Revelation of the Sin of Israel Under Law, Chapters 2:17—3:8
         (d) Revelation of the Universality of Sin, Chapter 3:9–20
             (1) Judge's Verdict of Guilty Against Mankind, Chapter 3:9–12
                 *(Man cannot remove guilt.)*

# CHAPTER 1

*THEME:* Paul's personal greetings; Paul's purpose;
Paul's three "I ams"; a natural revelation of God;
subnatural response of man; unnatural retrogression
of man

This opening chapter is an inclusive as it embraces the introduction, the missionary motives of the great apostle, the definition of the gospel, and the condition of man in sin which necessitates the gospel. This chapter furnishes the tempo for the entire epistle.

Romans teaches the total depravity of man. Man is irrevocably and hopelessly lost. He must have the righteousness of God since he has none of his own.

It is interesting to note that this great document of Christian doctrine, which was addressed to the church at Rome to keep it from heresy, did not accomplish its purpose. The Roman church moved the farthest from the faith which is set forth in the Epistle to the Romans. It is an illustration of the truth of this epistle that man does not understand, neither does he seek after God.

Verses 16 and 17 have long been recognized as the key to the epistle. These two verses should be memorized and the meaning of each word digested. The words will be dealt with individually when we come to them.

## PAUL'S PERSONAL GREETINGS

**Paul, a servant of Jesus Christ, called to be an apostle,
separated unto the gospel of God [Rom. 1:1].**

The name *Paul* comes from the Latin *Paulus,* meaning "little." (He was Saul of Tarsus but was also called Paul as indicated by Acts 13:9).

Paul identified himself to the Romans in the very beginning as a slave, or *doulos,* of the Lord Jesus Christ. He took the position of a servant willingly. The Lord Jesus Christ loved us and gave Himself for us, but He never makes us His slaves. You must come voluntarily to Him and make yourself His slave. He will never force you to serve Him. He said even to Jerusalem, "O Jerusalem, Jerusalem, which killest the prophets, and stonest them that are sent unto thee; how often would I have gathered thy children together, as a hen doth gather her brood under her wings, and ye would not!" (Luke 13:34). On another occasion our Lord said, "And ye will not come to me, that ye might have life" (John 5:40). It is wonderful beyond measure that you have the privilege of making yourself a bondslave to the Lord Jesus Christ. You must do it on your own; He will not force you.

On the road to Damascus, the Lord said to Paul, "Saul, Saul, why persecutest thou me?" And Paul replied, "Who art thou, Lord?" He said, "I am Jesus whom thou persecutest." It was at this moment that Paul came to know Him as his Savior. Then Paul's question was, "What wilt thou have me to do?" (see Acts 9:4–6). This is when Paul made himself a bondslave of the Lord Jesus Christ.

"Paul, a servant of Jesus Christ, called to be an apostle"—the infinitive of the verb "to be" is not in the original manuscripts. Paul was a "called apostle"—*called* is an adjective—he means that he is that kind of an apostle. It was not his decision that made him an apostle. It was God's decision, and God called him. Paul first made himself a bondslave of Christ, and now he is a called apostle, a witness for the Lord Jesus Christ. One whom He has chosen is the only kind of servant God will use. There are too many men in the ministry today whom God has not called. Paul could say, ". . . woe is unto me, if I preach not the gospel!" (1 Cor. 9:16). You may remember that Jeremiah was called when he was a child (Jer. 1:4–10). God said of the false prophets, "I have not sent these prophets, yet they ran: I have not spoken to them, yet they prophesied" (Jer. 23:21). Jeremiah was a called prophet, and Paul was a called apostle.

Paul says that he is an apostle, which means "one who is sent." Our Lord said that he that is sent [apostle] is not greater than he that sent him (see John 13:16). The same word occurs again in Philippians 2:25. The word has the technical meaning in the New Testament of one chosen by the Lord Jesus to declare the gospel. He must be a witness of the resurrected Christ. Paul said that the resurrected Christ had appeared to him. "And last of all he was seen of me also, as of one born out of due time" (1 Cor. 15:8). Then Paul asks the rhetorical question, "Am I not an apostle? am I not free? have I not seen Jesus Christ our Lord? . . ." (1 Cor. 9:1).

Another evidence that Paul was an apostle was that he had what we call "sign gifts." He said that he could speak other languages, other tongues. I believe that when he went through the Galatian country, for instance, into that area along the Aegean Sea where there were so many Greek cities and tribes in which unfamiliar languages were spoken, Paul was able to speak the language of each tribe as he came among them. He had the apostolic gift of tongues. Also he had the gift of healing, a gift that I do not believe is in existence today. When God heals in our day, He does it directly. I tell folk that I take my case directly to the Great Physician, not to one of the interns. I know that God heals, but He does not give that *gift* to men in our day. However, Paul had the gift of healing; he was an apostle. He could also raise the dead. We have records of both Peter and Paul raising the dead. They were apostles.

Now, Paul is a bondslave of Jesus Christ; he is a called apostle; and he is "separated unto the gospel of God." Notice that "separated" is used with the preposition *unto*, not *from*. He was separated unto the gospel of God.

The word *separated* is a marvelous word. There are several words that have almost an opposite meaning. For instance, there is the word *cleave*. An object can cleave to something or an object can be cleaved asunder. One time *cleave* can mean to join together and another time it can mean to separate. Paul was a separated Christian, but he was separated *to* something, not *from* something. I am afraid that many Christians today are only separated from something. When I hear some people talk, I get the idea that they are doing a spiritual striptease. They say, "I don't do this and I don't do that anymore." Well, my friend, *unto* what are you separated? Paul tells us that the Thessalonians turned to God from idols. They did not get up in a testimonial meeting and say, "We do not go to the temple of Apollo anymore." There was no need to say that because they were separated unto the

Lord Jesus Christ. A Christian who is separated *from* something and not separated *unto* Christ will have a barren life. His life will be without joy, and he will become critical and sometimes cynical. A phrase in the marriage ceremony I use says, "Do you promise to love and to keep yourself unto her (or him) and no one else?" This is separation unto one person. That is what marriage is. Imagine a fellow on the first night of his honeymoon saying to his new bride, "I have a girlfriend in this town. I think I will go to see her." There are many Christians who practice that kind of "separation"! If you are separated unto Christ, you will have a life that appeals rather than one that turns people off. A little Chinese girl once said, "Christians are salt. Salt makes you thirsty." Think it over, friend. Do you make anyone thirsty for Christ, the Water of Life?

The word *separated* is the Greek word *aphorizō*, the same word from which we get our word *horizon*. I have noticed when taking off on a plane that the horizon becomes enlarged. I remember a flight from Athens, Greece. When we took off, I tried to see the Acropolis and the ocean, but I could not see a thing. We had not gone far when I could see the ocean, the Acropolis, the outer islands, and the mountains. The higher we flew, the wider was the horizon. It is wonderful to be separated unto Christ because He brings you to the place where your horizons are enlarged. This is what Paul is talking about in 1 Corinthians 13:11 when he says, "When I was a child, I spake as a child, I understood as a child, I thought as a child: but when I became a man, I put away childish things."

I can recall a time in my early boyhood when I used to play house. Because there was a bunch of girls in the neighborhood and only a couple of boys, in order to play, we played house with the girls. There came a day, friend, when I outgrew that stuff, and I went outside and played baseball. The girls would say, "Let's play house." I would reply, "No, I am playing first base on the team. I am not interested in playing house anymore." I had a new horizon. Today I am not only uninterested in playing baseball, I *can't* play baseball. But I am interested in something else. My horizons have widened. And, friend, when you are separated unto Christ, it doesn't mean you become little and narrow. Rather, life broadens out to include innumerable thrilling and wonderful experiences.

Now notice that Paul says he is separated unto "the gospel of *God.*" In other words, man did not create the gospel. When you and I arrived on the scene, the gospel had been in existence for over nineteen hundred years. He didn't wait until we got here to see if we had a better plan. It is God's gospel. We can take it or leave it. The gospel was originated by God.

**(Which he had promised afore by his prophets in the holy scriptures,) [Rom. 1:2].**

The gospel is not brand new. It was promised by His prophets all the way through the Old Testament. It is a message that God loves mankind and that God presents a way of saving mankind. It brings us into a love relationship. He loves us and gave Himself for us. How wonderful!

Verses 2–6 form a parenthesis which gives a definition of the gospel. First of all, it is all about Jesus Christ.

**Concerning his Son Jesus Christ our Lord, which was made of the seed of David according to the flesh [Rom. 1:3].**

The word *concerning* is the little Greek preposition *peri*—used also in *periscope* and *perimeter*—and means "that which encircles." The gospel is all about Jesus Christ. It is what He has done. It is "concerning his Son Jesus Christ our Lord."

We have His full title here. He is the Son of God, and He is Jesus Christ our Lord. That is His wonderful name. We often hear today that we need the religion of Jesus. My friend, He had no religion. He didn't need one—He is God. What we need today is to have a religion that is *about* Jesus, that surrounds Him, that is all about what He has done. Jesus Christ actually is God. He cannot worship; He is to be worshiped. Somebody objects, "But He prayed." Yes, because He took the place of humanity. He prayed as a means of accommodation. For instance, at the grave of Lazarus the Bible says, ". . . Jesus lifted up his eyes, and said, Father, I thank thee that thou hast heard me. And I knew that thou hearest me always: but because of the people which stand by I said it, that they may believe that thou hast sent me" (John 11:41–42). My friend, He prayed to help our faith, but He is the Lord Jesus Christ.

Notice that He also is of the seed (the sperm) of David, according to the flesh. This is the humanity of Jesus. He is virgin-born because He is declared—horizoned out to be—the Son of God with power.

> **And declared to be the Son of God with power, according to the spirit of holiness, by the resurrection from the dead [Rom. 1:4].**

You see, the Resurrection did not make Him the Son of God; it simply revealed who He was.

*Declared* is from the same Greek word *horizo*, which we have seen before. Jesus is declared, He is horizoned, the Son of God. This gives us the perfect humanity of Christ and the perfect deity of Christ. One of the oldest creeds in the church states that He is very man of very man and that He is very God of very God. And Paul said it before the creed was written. Here it is. Jesus Christ is not any more man because He is God, and He is not any less God because He is man. He is God-man.

He is declared to be the Son of God "according to the spirit of holiness." This could mean the human spirit of Jesus, but I personally believe the reference is to the Holy Spirit. I believe the Trinity is in view here.

Now notice that He is declared to be the Son of God "by the resurrection from the dead." The Resurrection proves everything. It is Resurrection that sets Him forth as the Son of God. As you read through the Bible you will discover that the Lord Jesus Christ is presented in the power of His resurrection. First He is seen in the days of His flesh, walking upon the earth, despised and rejected of men. He is seen even in weakness as He sits down to rest at a well and as He sleeps through a storm on the sea. And He finally is brought to ignominy and shame and death upon a cross. Although He was a Man of Sorrows and acquainted with grief, there came a time when He was raised from the dead. His resurrection proves that He was accurate when He said, ". . . Ye are from beneath; I am from above: ye are of this world; I am not of this world" (John 8:23). The days of walking along the dusty roads of Israel are over now; He has come back from the dead in mighty power. His resurrection proves His virgin birth. He is the Son of God with power.

Then there is another great truth here. We see Christ, resurrected and presently seated at the right hand of God in the heavens, interceding today for believers and giving them power and comfort. There is a Man in the glory, but the church has lost sight of Him. We need to recover our awareness of Him. Are you having personal contact with the living Christ today?

Also the resurrection of Christ insures that He will return to this earth as the Judge and as the King of kings and Lord of lords. He will put down sin, and He will reign in righteousness on this earth. He will judge mankind, as Paul said to those glib, sophisticated Athenian philosophers, ". . . we ought not to think that the Godhead is like unto gold, or silver, or stone, graven by art and man's device. And the times of this ignorance God winked at; but now commandeth all men everywhere to repent: because he hath appointed a day, in which he will judge the world in righteousness by that man whom he hath ordained; whereof he hath given assurance unto all men, in that he hath raised him from the dead" (Acts 17:29–31). It is a most solemn fact that because Jesus Christ came back from the dead, you will have to stand before Him someday. Will you stand before Him as one who has trusted Him as your Savior, or will you stand before Him to be judged? If you have not received Him as your Savior, the condemnation of God must be upon you. You cannot stand before Him in your own righteousness. You must be condemned to a lost eternity unless you trust Him as your Savior. The Resurrection is the guarantee that each one of us is going to have to face the Lord Jesus Christ.

**By whom we have received grace and apostleship, for obedience to the faith among all nations, for his name [Rom. 1:5].**

"Grace and apostleship" are significant terms. "Grace" is God's method of salvation. None of us could ever have been saved if God had not been gracious. Although "apostleship" referred specifically to Paul and the others who were technically apostles, every believer is a "sent one." The word in the Greek is *apostolē*, meaning "a sending forth." Every believer should be a witness, one sent forth with a message. What are you doing to get the Word of God out in these days? That is the business of those who have received grace and apostleship.

For the "obedience to the faith among all nations, for his name—this epistle opens with obedience and closes with obedience. In the final chapter Paul says, "For your obedience is come abroad unto all men" (Rom. 16:19), also "made known to all nations for the obedience of faith" (Rom. 16:26). Obedience to the faith is very important to God. God saves us by faith, not by works; but after He has saved us, He wants to talk to us about our works, about our obedience to Him. I hear many people talk about believing in Jesus, then they live like the Devil and seem to be serving him. My friend, saving faith makes you obedient to Jesus Christ.

Is there a difference in faith? There surely is. The difference is in the object of your faith. For example, I believe in George Washington. I consider him a great man, our first president, the father of our country. Also, I believe in Jesus Christ. Now my faith in George Washington has never done anything for me. It has nothing to do with my salvation and has very little effect upon my life. But my faith in the Lord Jesus Christ is quite different. "Saving faith" brings us to the place where we *surrender* to the Son of God who loves us and gave Himself for us. While correct doctrine is very important, there is a discipline and a *doing* that goes with it. You can't be the salt of the earth without combining both of them. By the way, have you ever considered that salt is composed of sodium and chloride, and each taken by itself would poison you? However, when they are combined, they form a very useful ingredient. Believing and doing go together, my friend, to make us the salt of the earth. My favorite hymn has always been "Trust and Obey," by Rev. J. H. Sammis.

> But we never can prove
> The delights of His love,
> Until all on the altar we lay,
> For the favor He shows,
> And the joy He bestows,
> Are for them who will trust and obey.
>
> Trust and obey, for there's no other way
> To be happy in Jesus, but to trust and obey.

**Among whom are ye also the called of Jesus Christ [Rom. 1:6].**

The called are the elect. Who are the called? Well, they are those who have heard. The Lord Jesus made it clear when He said, "My sheep hear my voice, and I know them, and they follow me" (John 10:27). If you are following someone or something else, you haven't heard Him, you are not one of His sheep. The ones who hear and follow Him are the called ones. Let's not argue about election. It is as simple as this: He calls, and you answer. If you have answered, you are among the elect, one of "the called of Jesus Christ." Paul assures the Roman Christians that they are called ones.

This concludes the profound parenthesis in the introduction to this letter to the Romans. Dr. James Stifler calls our attention to four features of this parenthesis: Paul has a message in accord with the Scriptures; the message is from the risen Christ; the message is universal; and the message is for the obedience to the faith.

Now Paul returns to the introduction proper:

**To all that be in Rome, beloved of God, called to be saints: Grace to you and peace from God our Father, and the Lord Jesus Christ [Rom. 1:7].**

"Beloved of God"—isn't that lovely? God loved those believers in Rome. When I was there not long ago, there was a strike going on, and I found it a little difficult to love anybody as I was carrying my own suitcases up to my room and unable to get any kind of service—even a taxi. But God loves us. How wonderful!

"Called to be saints" should be simply "called saints"—the verb *to be* is not in the better manuscripts. They were "called saints" and this is the name for every believer. A saint is not one who has been exalted; a saint is one who exalts Jesus Christ. A person becomes a saint when Jesus Christ becomes his Savior. There are only two classes of people in the world: the saints and the ain'ts. If you are not an ain't, then you're a saint. And if you are a saint, you have trusted Christ. It is not your character that makes you a saint, it's your faith in Jesus Christ and the fact that you are set apart for Him. As Paul said of himself in the beginning, he was a bondslave of Jesus Christ.

"Grace and peace" constitute the formal introduction in all of Paul's letters. Grace (*charis*) was the gentile form of greeting, while peace (*shalom*) was the Jewish form of greeting. Paul combined them.

## PAUL'S PURPOSE

**First, I thank my God through Jesus Christ for you all, that your faith is spoken of throughout the whole world [Rom. 1:8].**

Word had filtered out throughout the empire that many in Rome were turning to Christ—so much so that it disturbed the emperors. Later on, persecution began. Paul mentions here that their faith was spoken of throughout the whole world.

I wonder about your group, your church. Has anybody heard about your personal testimony? What is it worth today? My, what a testimony this church in Rome had at the beginning!

**For God is my witness, whom I serve with my spirit in the gospel of his Son, that without ceasing I make mention of you always in my prayers [Rom. 1:9].**

"The gospel of his Son"—in the first verse Paul called it "the gospel of God," and later he will call it his gospel.

"Without ceasing I make mention of you always in my prayers." Paul had a long prayer list. When I was teaching in a Bible institute, I gave the students the assignment of recording each time Paul said he was praying for somebody. Many of the students were deeply impressed at the length of Paul's prayer list. He says here that he prayed without ceasing for the Roman believers.

> **Making request, if by any means now at length I might have a prosperous journey by the will of God to come unto you [Rom. 1:10].**

Paul is praying for a "prosperous journey" to come to Rome. When we read about his journey in the Book of Acts, it doesn't look exactly prosperous—he went as a prisoner, he got into a terrific storm at sea, the ship was lost, and he was bitten by a viper when he made it to land. Yet it was a prosperous journey.

He says he wants to come to Rome "by the will of God." I believe he went there by the *will* of God.

> **For I long to see you, that I may impart unto you some spiritual gift, to the end ye may be established [Rom. 1:11].**

He wants to come to Rome to teach the Word of God. Paul loved to teach the Word of God. When a preacher does not want to teach the Word of God, he becomes a clergyman, he becomes an administrator, he becomes a promoter, but he is not a minister of the Word anymore. I know several men in this position. One man said, "I don't enjoy preaching anymore." I said, "For goodness sake, get out of the ministry. You have no business in the ministry if you don't love to teach the Word of God!"

> **That is, that I may be comforted together with you by the mutual faith both of you and me [Rom. 1:12].**

In other words, Paul would communicate something, but the believers in Rome would also communicate something to him. They would be mutually blessed in the Word. Not too long ago I had the privilege of speaking to a conference of over a thousand students. I laid it on the line for those folk and was a little hard on them at the beginning. Then I saw how wonderfully they responded, and it opened my eyes to a new world. I left that conference singing praises to God for the privilege of being there. While I was ministering to them, they were ministering to me. This is what Paul is talking about here.

> Now I would not have you ignorant, brethren, that often-
> times I purposed to come unto you, (but was let hith-
> erto,) that I might have some fruit among you also, even
> as among other Gentiles [Rom. 1:13].

He was hindered from coming to them, although he longed to come. Many of these folk were his converts, as he had led them to Christ when he had met them in different parts of the Roman Empire. His desire to have "fruit among you" probably does not refer to soul winning, but to the fruit of the Spirit in the lives of believers (see Gal. 5:22–23).

### PAUL'S THREE "I AMS"

**I am debtor both to the Greeks, and to the Barbarians; both to the wise, and to the unwise [Rom. 1:14].**

"To the Greeks, and to the Barbarians" was the Greek division of all mankind. The Greeks were cultured, educated, and civilized. The barbarians were those whom we label pagan and heathen today. Actually, it is a false division, but it encompasses all mankind and was understood by Romans.

Paul said, "I am debtor both to the Greeks, and to the Barbarians." How did he become indebted? Did he run up a bill for neckties and shoes (that is what Rome is famous for today) and forget to pay the bill? No, he had had no business transaction with these people. However, he had had a personal transaction with Jesus Christ which put

him in debt to every man, because the grace of God had been so boun-
tifully bestowed upon him. Paul was in debt to a lost world. I hear
Christians say, "I pay my honest debts." Do you? Not until *every person* has heard the gospel of Jesus Christ have you and I paid our honest
debts. One day I was driving with a preacher friend of mine in the
interior of Turkey. (Turkey is closed to the gospel—a person can get
into trouble even propagandizing there.) As we were driving along,
we came to a little town in which all of the signs were in Turkish, and
we felt very much like strangers in a strange land. Then way down at
the end of the street we saw a big sign which read: *"Coca-Cola."* I said
to my friend, "Is it not interesting that *Coca-Cola* in just a few years
has done a better job of advertising and getting out its message than
has been done with the gospel in over nineteen hundred years?" We
have not paid our debt, friend, until all have heard the good news, and
multitudes have not yet heard. Paul says, "I am debtor," and that was
another reason he wanted to come to Rome.

Then Paul has another "I am."

> **So, as much as in me is, I am ready to preach the gospel
> to you that are at Rome also [Rom. 1:15].**

Paul has said that he is a debtor; now he says he is ready to pay. In
other words, Paul says, "My side is ready." In *The Epistle to the Romans* Dr. James Stifler writes, "He is a master of his purpose, but not
of his circumstances." He is not only ready, he is eager to preach it.
Oh, how we need that enthusiasm and high anticipation of getting out
the Word of God!

In the next verse we have the third "I am" of Paul. Also verses 16
and 17 give us the key to this great Epistle to the Romans.

> **For I am not ashamed of the gospel of Christ: for it is the
> power of God unto salvation to every one that believeth;
> to the Jew first, and also to the Greek [Rom. 1:16].**

"I am not ashamed of the gospel" ("of Christ" is not in the better
manuscripts). Paul says, "I am debtor. . . . I am ready. . . . I am not

ashamed." I am a debtor—that is admission; I am ready—remission; I am not ashamed—submission. These are the three "missions" of Paul: admission, remission, and submission.

Why did Paul say, "I am not ashamed of the gospel"? As I walked down the streets of Ephesus and looked at the ruins of marble temples, I realized that there was not a church building in Ephesus in the first century. In Ephesus was one of the seven wonders of the ancient world, the gorgeous temple of Diana (or Artemis), but there was no church building. I suppose there were folk in Rome who were saying, "Well, brother Paul hasn't come to Rome because he is just preaching a message geared for poor people. The message he preaches is without prestige; there are no great temples connected with it. He would be ashamed to bring it to an important place like Rome." So Paul says, "I am not ashamed of the gospel."

Now why is Paul not ashamed of the gospel? "It is the power of God"! The Greek word translated "power" is *dunamis*, from which we get our word *dynamite*. It is *dunamis* power! It is the kind of power Dr. Marvin R. Vincent calls divine energy! In itself the gospel has power, innate power.

It has power for a very definite thing: "It is the power of God unto salvation." That is the end and the effect of the gospel. "Salvation" is the all-inclusive term of the gospel, and it simply means "deliverance." It embraces everything from justification to glorification. It is both an act and a process. It is equally true that I *have* been saved, I *am* being saved, and I *shall be* saved.

The gospel is "to the Jew first, and also to the Greek." It's to everyone. It includes the entire human race, irrespective of racial or religious barriers. And it is personal; it is directed to every individual—"whosoever will may come."

It is universal in scope, but it is limited to "every one that believeth." This statement wraps up election and free will in one package. The only way of procuring salvation is by personal faith.

"To the Jew first, and also to the Greek" does not imply that the Jew has top priority to the gospel today. The important thing is to make sure the Jew is on a par with the Gentile as far as evangelism is concerned. Chronologically the gospel went to the Jew first. If you had been in Jerusalem on the Day of Pentecost, you would have seen an altogether Jewish meeting. And Paul in his missionary journeys took the gospel first to the Jewish synagogue, but in Acts 13:46 we are told, "Then Paul and Barnabas waxed bold, and said, It was necessary that the word of God should first have been spoken to you: but seeing ye put it from you, and judge yourselves unworthy of everlasting life, lo, we turn to the Gentiles." The gospel began in Jerusalem, a Jewish city, then spread to Judea, Samaria, and to the ends of the earth.

Dr. Stifler calls our attention to three very pertinent truths in this verse: the effect of the gospel—salvation; the extent—it is worldwide—to everyone; the condition—faith in Jesus Christ.

> **For therein is the righteousness of God revealed from faith to faith: as it is written, The just shall live by faith [Rom. 1:17].**

"A righteousness from God is being revealed" is a literal translation. It should not be *the* righteousness of God, because that would be His attribute, and God is not sharing His attribute with anyone. It is *a* righteousness, and it is from God; it is not man's righteousness. God has already said that He will not accept the righteousness of man, for the righteousness of man is as filthy rags in His sight according to Isaiah 64:6. Paul is talking about the imputed righteousness of Christ. God places a lost sinner in Christ, and He sees him in Christ. The believer is absolutely accepted because of what Christ has done for him. The only method of procuring this righteousness is by faith. It is a by-faith righteousness. You can't work for it; you can't make a deposit on it; you can't buy it. You can do nothing but accept it by faith. "And be found in him, not having mine own righteousness, which is of the law, but that which is through the faith of Christ, the righteousness which is of God by faith" (Phil. 3:9).

The word for "righteousness" is *dikaiosune*. This word occurs ninety-two times in the New Testament, thirty-six times in Romans. The phrase "a righteousness from God" occurs eight times in this epistle. The root word *dike* means simply "right." *Justice* and *justify* come from the same word. "To be right" is the primary meaning, which is the antonym of sin. Dr. Cremer gives this apt definition: "It is the state commanded by God and standing the test of His judgment; the character and acts of a man approved of Him, in virtue of which the man corresponds with Him and His will as His ideal and standard." The righteousness he is talking about is what God demands, and it is what God provides—it is a righteousness that is from God.

"From faith to faith" simply means out of faith into faith. God saves you by faith, you live by faith, you die by faith, and you'll be in heaven by faith. Let me use a homely illustration. Quite a few years ago I was born deep in the heart of Texas. When I was born, my mother said the doctor lifted me up by my heels, gave me a whack, and I let out a cry that could be heard on all four borders of that great state. I was born into a world of atmosphere and that whack started me breathing. From that day to this I have been breathing atmosphere. From air to air, from oxygen to oxygen. Much later, in the state of Oklahoma, I was born again. I was saved by faith, and from that time on it has been by faith—from faith to faith.

"As it is written" refers to Habakkuk 2:4, where the statement is made, ". . . the just shall live by his faith." This is quoted in three great epistles of the New Testament: Romans, Galatians, and Hebrews.

"The just shall live by faith"—justification by faith means that a sinner who trusts Christ is not only pardoned because Christ died, but he also stands before God complete in Christ. It means not only subtraction of sin, but addition of righteousness. He "was delivered for our offences, and was raised again for our justification" (Rom. 4:25)—that we might stand before God complete in Christ.

The act of God in justification by faith is not an arbitrary decision on His part. He does not disregard His holiness and His justice. Since God saves us by grace, this means that there is no merit in us. He saves us on no other ground than that we trust Jesus. God is in danger of impugning His own justice if the penalty is not paid. He is not going to open the back door to heaven and slip sinners in under cover of darkness. But because He loves you, Christ died for you to make a way. The Lord Jesus Christ is the way to heaven. Since Christ paid the penalty for our sin, salvation is ours "through faith in his blood" (Rom. 3:25). The hymn writer is correct—

> Jesus paid it all,
> All to Him I owe;
> Sin had left a crimson stain,
> He washed it white as snow.

This concludes Paul's introduction. Now he begins a new section in which he reveals the sin of man. My friend, this is "sinnerama." The universal fact is that man is a sinner. The ecumenical movement is always *away* from God. We can put down the axiom that the world is guilty before God; all need righteousness. In this section Paul is not attempting to prove that man is a sinner. If you attempt to read it that way, you will miss the point. All Paul is doing is stating the fact that man is a sinner. He not only shows that there is a revelation of the righteousness of God, but that there is also the revelation of the *wrath* of God against the sin of man.

## A NATURAL REVELATION OF GOD

**For the wrath of God is revealed from heaven against all ungodliness and unrighteousness of men, who hold the truth in unrighteousness [Rom. 1:18].**

"The *wrath* of God is revealed." Actually, if you want to know what salvation really is, you have to know how bad sin is. Stifler says, "Sin is the measure of salvation." The wrath of God is God's feeling, not His punishment of sin. It is His holy anger. Wrath is the antithesis of righteousness, and it is used here as a correlative.

"Is being revealed" is God's answer to those who assert that the Old Testament presents a God of wrath, while the New Testament presents a God of love. There is a continuous revelation of the wrath of God in both the Old Testament and New Testament. It is revealed in our contemporary society. This is God's constant and insistent displeasure with evil. He changes not. God is merciful, not because He is lenient with the sinner, but because Christ died. The gospel has not changed God's attitude toward sin. The gospel has made it possible to accept the sinner. The sinner must have either the righteousness or the wrath of God. Both are revealed from heaven. And you can see it on every hand. If you want to know how bad sin is, look at the cases of venereal diseases today. You don't get by with sin, my friend. I won't give personal illustrations, but I have been a pastor long enough to see again and again the judgment of God upon sin. It is revealed from heaven. Also there will be a *final* judgment.

"Against all ungodliness"—ungodliness is that which is against God. It is that which denies the character of God. Oh, the irreligiousness of today! There are multitudes of people who disregard the very existence of God—that is a *state* of the soul. That is sin.

"Unrighteousness" is against man. Ungodliness is against God, but unrighteousness is against man. What does that mean? It is the denial of the rule of God. It is the *action* of the soul. That man who gets drunk, goes out on the freeway, breaks the traffic laws, and kills someone—that man is unrighteous. He is sinning against man. Another example is the man who is dishonest in his business dealings. God hates man's unrighteousness. He will judge it.

"Who holds the truth in unrighteousness" is literally to hold down, suppress the truth in unrighteousness. The wrath of God is revealed against folk who do this.

> **Because that which may be known of God is manifest in them; for God hath shewed it unto them [Rom. 1:19].**

There is an original revelation from God.

> **For the invisible things of him from the creation of the world are clearly seen, being understood by the things that are made, even his eternal power and Godhead; so that they are without excuse [Rom. 1:20].**

This universe in which you and I live tells two things about God: His person and His power. This has been clearly seen from the time the world was created. How can invisible things be seen? Paul makes this a paradox purposely to impress upon his readers that the "dim light of nature" is a man-made falsehood. Creation is a clear light of revelation. It is the primary revelation. The psalmist said, "When I consider thy heavens, the work of thy fingers, the moon and the stars, which thou hast ordained" (Ps. 8:3). Also "The heavens declare the glory of God; and the firmament sheweth his handiwork" (Ps. 19:1).

"His eternal power and Godhead"—His eternal power and deity, power and person. Creation reveals the unchangeable power and existence of God. Paul said this, ". . . he left not himself without witness, in that he did good, and gave us rain from heaven, and fruitful seasons, filling our hearts with food and gladness" (Acts 14:17). And because all of us are the offspring (not the sons) of God, Paul said, "Forasmuch then as we are the offspring of God, we ought not to think that the Godhead is like unto gold, or silver, or stone, graven by art and man's device" (Acts 17:29). Dr. James Denny writes, "There is that within man which so catches the meaning of all that is without as to issue in an instinctive knowledge of God." I think the most ridiculous position man can hold is that of atheism. It is illogical and senseless. When the psalmist said, "The fool hath said in his heart, There is no God" (Ps. 14:1), the word for *fool* means "insane." A man is insane when he denies the existence of God.

"So that they are without excuse." Creation so clearly reveals God that man is without excuse. This section reveals the historical basis of man's sin. It did not come about through ignorance. It was willful rebellion in the presence of clear light.

## SUBNATURAL RESPONSE OF MAN

If you examine the next few verses carefully, you will see that there are seven steps which mankind took downward from the Garden of Eden.

> **Because that, when they knew God, they glorified him not as God, neither were thankful; but became vain in their imaginations, and their foolish heart was darkened.**
>
> **Professing themselves to be wise, they became fools,**

**And changed the glory of the uncorruptible God into an image made like to corruptible man, and to birds, and fourfooted beasts, and creeping things [Rom. 1:21–23].**

There is no such thing as man moving upward. These verses contradict the hypothesis of evolution. Man is not improving physically, morally, intellectually, or spiritually. The pull is downward. Of course this contradicts all the anthologies of religion that start with man in a very primitive condition as a caveman with very little intellectual qualities and move him up intellectually and begin moving him toward God. This is absolute error. Man is moving away from God, and right now the world is probably farther from God than at any time in its history. The fact of the matter is that every primitive tribe has a tradition that way back in the beginning their ancestors knew God. Dr. Vincent in *Word Studies in the New Testament* says, "I think it may be proved from facts that any given people, down to the lowest savages, has at any period of its life known far more than it has done: known quite enough to have enabled it to have got on comfortably, thriven and developed, if it had only done what no man does, all that it knew it ought to do and could do." No people have ever lived up to the light that they have had. Although they had a knowledge of God, they moved away from Him.

"They glorified him not as God." They did not give Him His rightful place, and man became self-sufficient. In our day man has made the announcement that God is dead. In the beginning the human family did not suggest that God was dead, they simply turned their backs upon Him and made man their god.

"Neither were thankful." Ingratitude is one of the worst sins there is. You recall that the Lord Jesus healed ten lepers, but only one returned to thank Him. Only ten percent were thankful, and I believe it is less than that today.

"Became vain in their imaginations"—they even concocted a theory of evolution.

"Their foolish heart was darkened." They moved into the darkness of paganism. You see living proof of this as you walk down the streets of Cairo in Egypt or of Istanbul in Turkey. In fact, all you have to do is walk down the streets of Los Angeles to know that man's foolish heart is darkened.

"Professing themselves to be wise, they became fools." The wisdom of man is foolishness with God. Man searches for truth through logical reasoning but arrives at a philosophy that is foolish in God's sight.

"And changed the glory of the uncorruptible God into an image made like to corruptible man, and to birds, and fourfooted beasts, and creeping things." Have you noted that the unsaved world has made caricatures of God? Look at the images and the idols of the heathen. I was aware of this during my visit to the ruins of the ancient city of Ephesus. That city in the Roman Empire reached probably the highest degree of culture in civilization that any city has ever reached. Yet at the heart of that city was one of the most horrible images imaginable, enshrined in the temple of Artemis, one of the seven wonders of the ancient world. Called also Diana, she was not the lovely image you see in Greek sculptures. She is like the oriental Cybele, the mother goddess, the many-breasted one. She had a trident in one hand and in the other a club—she was a mean one. That is the idea the most cultured, civilized people had of God! She was a female principal, and gross immorality took place around her temple, and dishonesty of the worst sort. They had turned the glory of the uncorruptible God into the likeness of an image of corruptible man. Actually, idolatry is a cartoon of God; it is a slander and a slur against Him. Personally, I do not like to see pictures of Jesus, as Paul said that we know Him no longer after the flesh (see 2 Cor. 5:16). He is the glorified Christ. He is not that picture you have hanging on your wall, my friend. If He came into your room, you would fall on your face before Him. He is the glorified Christ today. Don't slur our God by having a picture of Him! The Greeks made their gods like men; the Assyrians and the Egyptians and the Babylonians made their gods like beasts and birds and creeping things. I walked through the museum in Cairo and looked at some of the gods they had made. They are not very flattering representations, I can assure you.

Man did not begin in idolatry. The savage of today is very unlike primitive man. Primitive man was monotheistic; idolatry was introduced later. In the Word of God the first record we have of idolatry is in connection with Rachel stealing her father's idols (Gen. 31). Man descended downward; he did not develop upward. Religiously man has departed from God. Sir William Ramsay, who was once a belligerent unbeliever, wrote in *The Cities of Paul:* "For my own part, I confess that my experience and reading show nothing to confirm the modern assumptions in religious history, and a great deal to confirm Paul. Whatever evidence exists, with the rarest exceptions, the history of religion among men is a history of degeneration. . . . Is it not the fact of human history that man, standing alone, degenerates; and that he progresses only where there is in him so much sympathy with and devotion to the Divine life as to keep the social body pure and sweet and healthy?" My friend, the reason today there is failure in our poverty programs and health programs and other social programs is because of gross immorality and a turning away from God. They say, "We want to be practical, and we do not want to introduce religion." That's the problem. The only *practical* thing for man to do is to return to the living and true God.

## UNNATURAL RETROGRESSION OF MAN

Now we see the results of man's revolution against God. In the remainder of this chapter it says three times that God gave them up.

> **Wherefore God also gave them up to uncleanness through the lusts of their own hearts, to dishonour their own bodies between themselves [Rom. 1:24].**

Man's degeneration is measured by his perversion of sex. While many churches in our day are espousing sex perversion instead of condemning it, God says He has given them up. Idolatry and gross immorality are the bitter fruits of rejecting God's revelation.

"God gave them up" is literally *God handed them over*—it is positive, not a passive attitude.

> Who changed the truth of God into a lie, and wor-
> shipped and served the creature more than the Creator,
> who is blessed for ever. Amen [Rom. 1:25].

"Who exchanged the true God for the lie." The suggestion is that they turned from God to Satan, the author of the lie and the father of idolatry. This is idolatry which led to the lowest depths of moral degradation.

> For this cause God gave them up unto vile affections: for
> even their women did change the natural use into that
> which is against nature:
>
> And likewise also the men, leaving the natural use of
> the woman, burned in their lust one toward another;
> men with men working that which is unseemly, and re-
> ceiving in themselves that recompence of their error
> which was meet [Rom. 1:26-27].

These are passions of dishonor and disgrace and depravity—regardless of what public opinion is today. Perversion entered into Greek life, and it brought Greece down to the dust. Go over there and look at Greece today. The glory has passed away. Why? These were their sins.

> And even as they did not like to retain God in their
> knowledge, God gave them over to a reprobate mind, to
> do those things which are not convenient [Rom. 1:28].

Anybody who tells me that he can be a child of God and live in perversion, live in the thick mire of our contemporary permissiveness, is not kidding anyone but himself. If he will come to Christ, he can have deliverance.

The next three verses list a frightful brood of sins which follow man's rebellion against God.

> Being filled with all unrighteousness, fornication, wickedness, covetousness, maliciousness; full of envy, murder, debate, deceit, malignity; whisperers,
>
> Backbiters, haters of God, despiteful, proud boasters, inventors of evil things, disobedient to parents,
>
> Without understanding, covenant-breakers, without natural affection, implacable, unmerciful [Rom. 1:29–31].

In my book *Reasoning Through Romans,* I define these sins, but it is enough to say here that this is what the human family is doing today. I used to tell the students in my classes to buy any of our metropolitan daily newspapers, sit down, and find a headline for every sin that is mentioned here. This is the condition, not only in Cairo, not only of Calcutta, not only of Beijing, but also of the United States today. How much longer will God tolerate it and be patient with us? He has judged great nations in the past who have gone in this direction.

> Who knowing the judgment of God, that they which commit such things are worthy of death, not only do the same, but have pleasure in them that do them [Rom. 1:32].

Man has a revelation from God, but he flagrantly flaunts it by defying the judgment of God against such sins. He continues to practice them and applauds and approves those who do the same.

# CHAPTER 2

*THEME:* God will judge self-righteous and religious people

In this chapter Paul is showing that God will judge self-righteous and religious people. There are many people like the man on the top of the hill who looks down at the man at the bottom of the hill and says, "Something should be done for that poor fellow. We ought to start a mission down there. We should start giving him soup and clothes and a shower bath. I am living on the top of the hill, and I do not need anything." The hurdle to meet the demands of God is just as high on top of the hill as it is at the bottom of the hill. The only difference is that the man at the bottom of the hill will probably see his need sooner than the man at the top of the hill. Religious people, self-righteous people, and so-called good people need a Savior. In chapter 2 Paul sets down certain principles by which God is going to judge "good" people. Chapter 1 reveals the unrighteousness of man, and chapter 2 reveals the self-righteousness of man.

> **Therefore thou art inexcusable, O man, whosoever thou art that judgest: for wherein thou judgest another, thou condemnest thyself; for thou that judgest doest the same things [Rom. 2:1].**

This puts before us the very important issue of this chapter. It's well to keep in mind here that Paul is not talking about salvation. He is talking about sin and the basis on which God will judge men. These principles of judgment are not the basis of salvation; they are the basis of judgment. I don't know about you, but I wouldn't want to be judged by them. I thank God for a Savior today, and Scripture presents the gospel as the only means of attaining eternal life. To reject the Son of God immediately brings upon a person the judgment of God, and the only verdict here is guilty. "He that hath the Son hath life; and he that hath not the Son of God hath not life" (1 John 5:12). And He says, "Verily, verily, I say unto you, He that heareth my word, and believeth on him that sent me, hath everlasting life, and shall not come into condemnation; but is passed from death unto life" (John 5:24). And then listen to the Lord Jesus after that marvelous, wonderful John 3:16—we generally stop there—but He continues: "For God sent not his Son into the world to condemn the world; but that the world through him might be saved. He that believeth on him is not condemned: but he that believeth not is condemned already, because he hath not believed in the name of the only begotten Son of God" (John 3:17–18). Also, "He that believeth on the Son hath everlasting life: and he that believeth not the Son shall not see life; but the wrath of God abideth on him" (John 3:36). So today these folk who do not have Christ are *lost*. You may be a religious person, you might be a good person, but without Christ, my friend, you're lost.

"Thou art inexcusable, O man"—"man" is the Greek *anthrope*, a generic term meaning both men and women. It includes both Jews and Gentiles and refers to mankind in general.

"Whosoever thou art that judgest." He passes now from the general to that which is specific, from the masses to the individual person. And he addresses any person of the human race, but he limits it to those who judge others. Now, the word here for "judge" carries the thought of judging with an adverse verdict. It can be translated, "Whosoever thou art that *condemnest* another." Therefore this raises the question: What should be the attitude of a believer today toward this awful, horrible group who are mentioned in Romans 1? It should be this: We should want them to get saved; we should try to get the gospel to them; they are poor, lost creatures. It should be as the hymn writer, Fanny Crosby, expressed it:

> Rescue the perishing,
> Care for the dying,
> Snatch them in pity from sin and the grave;
> Weep o'er the erring ones,
> Lift up the fallen,
> Tell them of Jesus, the mighty to save.

This should be our attitude, while making it clear that they need to be saved and delivered from perversion and immorality.

"For thou that judgest doest the same things" may give a wrong impression. "Same" is the Greek *auta*, and the meaning is not identical things, but things that are as bad in God's sight as the awful, depraved acts of the heathen which are offensive to the cultured and refined sinner.

Let me illustrate this. I heard a man who is not saved say that he didn't believe that hell could be heated hot enough for Hitler. My friend, he is sitting in judgment. He is taking the place of God. And you and I are sitting in judgment on those who are not on our plane. We use society's standards today, and it varies. If someone does not measure up to the standard of your little group, you condemn him. I know some churches where members can get by with lying, with being gossipers, and with being dishonest, but they couldn't get by with smoking a cigarette! They would be condemned for that. My friend, when you judge other people, you are assuming the position of judge. God is saying that by the same token that you have the right to judge other people by your standards, He has the right to judge you by His standards. If we could see ourselves as God sees us, we could see that we are obnoxious; we are repugnant! What contribution can you and I make to heaven? Would we adorn the place? I get the impression from some people that heaven is going to be a better place when they get there—yet the earth has not been a better place since they have been here! My friend, you try to deny God the same privilege you have of sitting in judgment on others. Well, God is going to judge you, and He won't judge you by your standards, but by *His* standards. Does that begin to move you? It ought to, because I have found that we don't come up to God's standards.

Now Paul puts down the principles by which God will judge the refined and cultured sinner. Here is the first great principle.

**But we are sure that the judgment of God is according to truth against them which commit such things [Rom. 2:2].**

In other words, he says, "We *know* that the judgment of God is according to reality." There are so many folk today, including church members, who live in a world of unreality. They do not want to hear the truth of the gospel. Now, I hear a great many pious folk who say, "Oh, I do want to study the Bible." And then when they get into the Word of God, they find what John found in the Book of Revelation when he began to see the judgments of God. When he first started out, it was thrilling, it was "sweet in his mouth." But when he ate that little book, it gave him indigestion, it was "bitter in his belly" (see Rev. 10:9–10). And there are a great many Christians today who say they want Bible study, but they don't want reality. They do not want to hear the truth. "We know that the judgment of God is according to reality [the factual condition of man] against them which commit such things."

Now keep in mine that these are principles of *judgment*, not principles of salvation. Man has an inherent knowledge that he must be judged by a higher power. The coming judgment of God is something every man out of Christ either dreads or denies. The Scripture is very clear on judgment. Paul said to the Athenians, "Because he hath appointed a day, in the which he will judge the world in righteousness by that man whom he hath ordained; whereof he hath given assurance unto all men, in that he hath raised him from the dead" (Acts 17:31). And Paul reasoned, you remember, with Felix about righteousness and self-control and judgment to come. And it frightened this fellow, Felix. In fact, he didn't want to hear another sermon. The judgment of God is in contrast with man's judgment. Man does not have all the facts and his judgment is partial and prejudiced. God's judgment takes in all the facts. God knows the actual state of man—just what he is. And on that basis He will judge him.

As a boy, I used to pick cotton—and I wasn't very good at it. I'd bring in a sack of cotton to be weighed, and they only weighed what I brought in. The man weighing the cotton didn't ask me where I picked it or how I picked it or to whom it belonged; he just weighed it. ". . . Thou art weighed in the balances . . ." (Dan. 5:27), is God's word to every man that boasts of his morality. I think the great delusion of the cultured person is that the depraved person must be judged, but he's confident that he will escape because he's different. Most people believe Hitler and Stalin ought to be judged, but they think they should escape. God will judge man for what he is in *His* sight. Do you want to stand before God on that basis? I don't.

> **And thinkest thou this, O man, that judgest them which do such things, and doest the same, that thou shalt escape the judgment of God? [Rom. 2:3].**

Robert Govett has called attention to the *four* ways of escape which are open to the man who breaks human laws:

1. His offence will not be discovered.
2. He may escape beyond the jurisdiction of the court.
3. After arrest, there may be some legal technicality which will cause a breakdown of the legal procedure.
4. After conviction, he may escape from prison and stay under cover.

None of these avenues of escape are open to man in regard to divine judgment. Your offenses will be discovered. You cannot go beyond God's jurisdiction. There will be no legal technicality. You will never be able to escape from prison. The writer of Hebrews asked, "How shall we escape, if we neglect so great salvation . . . ?" (Heb. 2:3).

> **Or despisest thou the riches of his goodness and forbearance and longsuffering; not knowing that the goodness of God leadeth thee to repentance? [Rom. 2:4].**

We ought to recognize today that the *goodness* of God is something that ought to bring us to our knees before Him. But instead of that, it drives men from God. David was disturbed by the way the wicked could prosper. God didn't seem to do anything to them. In Psalm 73, David says, "For I was envious at the foolish, when I saw the prosperity of the wicked. For there are no bands in their death: but their strength is firm. They are not in trouble as other men; neither are they plagued like other men. . . . They set their mouth against the heavens, and their tongue walketh through the earth. . . . Until I went into the sanctuary of God; then understood I their end" (Ps. 73:3–5, 9, 17). They will face God's judgment, my friend.

And, by the way, if you're a lost man, don't think I am the sort of preacher that tries to take everything away from you. If you haven't trusted Christ and your only hope is in this life, brother, you had better suck this earth like it is an orange and get all you can out of it. Drink all you can, sin all you can, because you won't have anything in the next life. You had better get it while you are here if that's the way you want to live. Eat, drink, and be merry. Tomorrow you die. My friend, you need a Savior. And the goodness of God ought to lead you to Him.

**But after thy hardness and impenitent heart treasurest up unto thyself wrath against the day of wrath and revelation of the righteous judgment of God [Rom. 2:5].**

If you are not saved, let me say this to you: you *know* God has been good to you. God has blessed you. Think of the multitudes of folk on this earth who have nothing, who are literally starving to death. And here you are, a wicked man, living on top of the world. Do you think God is not going to judge you? Do you think that you are going to escape? My friend, the very goodness of God ought to lead you to repentance.

As we come to verse 6, we see the second great principle.

**Who will render to every man according to his deeds [Rom. 2:6].**

He shall reward every man according to his works. Absolute justice is the criterion of the judgment or rewards. Man's deeds stand before God in His holy light. No man in his right mind wants to be judged on this basis. Remember Cornelius—he was a good man, but he was lost.

**To them who by patient continuance in well-doing seek for glory and honour and immorality, eternal life [Rom. 2:7].**

Let's keep in mind that under this second principle, a way of life is not the subject. Rather, a way of life is the basis of judgment. The "do-gooder" will be judged according to his works. John said, "And I saw the dead, small and great, stand before God; and the books were opened: and another book was opened, which is the book of life: and the dead were judged out of those things which were written in the books, according to their works" (Rev. 20:12). The man who wants to work for eternal life may do so. He will be judged according to his deeds, but he is warned that they will avail nothing. "And whosoever was not found written in the book of life was cast into that lake of fire" (Rev. 20:15). Trusting Christ as Savior puts your name in the "book of life." Eternal life is not a reward for effort; it is a gift to those who trust Christ.

Now notice the third principle of judgment.

**For there is no respect of persons with God [Rom. 2:11].**

This was also a great principle of the Old Testament. "For the LORD your God is God of gods, and Lord of lords, a great God, a mighty, and a terrible, which regardeth not persons, nor taketh reward" (Deut. 10:17). Simon Peter, discovered this when he went into the home of Cornelius. "Then Peter opened his mouth, and said, Of a truth I perceive that God is no respector of persons" (Acts 10:34). God plays no favorites. He has no pets. All men are alike before Him. Justice is blindfolded, not because she is blind, but that she may not see men in either silk or rags; all must appear alike. Church membership, a good family, being an outstanding citizen, or having a fundamental creed give no advantage before God at all. Do you have a Savior, or don't you? That is the all-important issue.

**For as many as have sinned without law shall also perish without law: and as many as have sinned in the law shall be judged by the law [Rom. 2:12].**

This is another great principle by which God is going to judge. Notice how it is expressed in the next verse.

**(For not the hearers of the law are just before God, but
the doers of the law shall be justified [Rom. 2:13].**

I hear it said that the heathen are lost because they haven't heard of
Christ and haven't accepted Him. My friend, they are lost because
they are sinners. That's the condition of all mankind. Men are not
*saved* by the light they have; they are *judged* by the light they have.

"For not the hearers of the law are just before God"—many folk
seem to think that if they just *approve* the Sermon on the Mount, they
are saved.

Now here is the fifth principle.

**Which shew the work of the law written in their hearts,
their conscience also bearing witness, and their
thoughts the mean while accusing or else excusing one
another;) [Rom. 2:15].**

God can and will judge the heathen by his own conscience. Some folk
think because the heathen do not have the revelation of God that they
will escape God's judgment. But the fact is that they are not living up
to the light they have. God will judge them on that basis.

**In the day when God shall judge the secrets of men by
Jesus Christ according to my gospel [Rom. 2:16].**

We have a false idea today that because we happen to be good folk,
that is, we think we are, that we'll be saved. God is going to *judge* the
do-gooders. And He will judge them by Jesus Christ who said that if a
man looks upon a woman to lust after her, he is guilty of adultery (see
Matt. 5:27–28). This is only one example of the secrets of the human
heart. Do you want the secrets of your heart brought out—not the
lovely things you have said, but the dirty little thoughts that come to
you? This should cause all of us to flee to Jesus to save us!

God is going to judge religious people, the Jews in particular, because theirs was a God-given religion.

**Behold, thou art called a Jew, and restest in the law, and
makest thy boast of God,**

> **And knowest his will, and approvest the things that are more excellent, being instructed out of the law [Rom. 2:17–18].**

Religion was no longer a crutch for this man. It caused him to be proud and self-sufficient. Light created an added responsibility, which brought a greater condemnation. The Jew had ten advantages over the Gentiles, which are listed in these verses. The first five are what he *was:* (1) bears the name Jew; (2) rests upon the law; (3) boasts in God; (4) knows the will of God; (5) proves the things which are more excellent, being instructed out of the Law.

> **And art confident that thou thyself art a guide of the blind, a light of them which are in darkness,**

> **An instructor of the foolish, a teacher of babes, which hast the form of knowledge and of the truth in the law [Rom. 2:19–20].**

The last five personal privileges of the Jew are what he *did:* (1) Art persuaded that thou thyself art a guide of the blind; (2) a light of them that are in darkness; (3) a corrector of the thoughtless or immature; (4) a teacher of babes or proselytes; and (5) having in the Law the outward form of knowledge and truth.

Now here is Paul's question:

> **Thou therefore which teachest another, teachest thou not thyself? thou that preachest a man should not steal, dost thou steal?**

> **Thou that sayest a man should not commit adultery, dost thou commit adultery? thou that abhorrest idols, dost thou commit sacrilege? [Rom. 2:21–22].**

Paul mentions three common sins: (1) immorality—sin against others; (2) sensuality—sin against self; and (3) idolatry—sin against God.

"Teachest thou not thyself?" In other words, "Do you practice what you preach?" For many of us our preaching is better than our living.

"Dost thou commit sacrilege?"—or "Do you rob temples?" When the Jew was in Babylonian captivity, he took "the gold cure," and, as far as I can tell, he was never given to idolatry after that. However, he didn't mind handling merchandise that came from heathen temples and selling it in his business. Today there are certain Christians who handle merchandise in their business (in order to make money) that they would condemn in their church.

Now the three sins that Paul mentions—immorality, sensuality, and idolatry—he had dealt with in inverse order in chapter 1. Idolatry was the terrible climax for the Jew; he could go no lower than that. I wonder if you and I make a mockery of the person of Christ. Someone has put the question in poetic language:

> The gospel is written a chapter a day
>   By deeds that you do and words that you say.
> Men read what you say, whether faithless or true,
>   Say, what is the gospel according to you?

Now he deals with something that is extremely vital.

**For circumcision verily profiteth, if thou keep the law: but if thou be a breaker of the law, thy circumcision is made uncircumcision [Rom. 2:25].**

Circumcision was the badge of the Mosiac system—and that's all it was. There was no merit in the rite itself. That badge indicated that the man believed the Mosaic Law. Now for them to be transgressors of the Law brought circumcision into disrepute. That which should have been sacred, became profane.

This thought can be applied to our church sacraments. Water baptism is rightly a sacrament of the church, *if* it is the outward expression of a work of God in the heart. But it is a mockery if the person who is baptized gives no evidence of salvation. This also can be said of church membership. The lives of some church members make membership a mockery.

Listen to Paul as he continues:

> **Therefore if the uncircumcision keep the righteousness of the law, shall not his uncircumcision be counted for circumcision? [Rom. 2:26].**

To use another figure of speech, if my wife loses her wedding ring, that does not mean she becomes unmarried. Marriage is more than a wedding ring, although the ring may be the symbol of it.

> **And shall not uncircumcision which is by nature, if it fulfill the law, judge thee, who by the letter and circumcision dost transgress the law? [Rom. 2:27].**

Using again the illustration of a wedding ring, to wear a wedding ring speaks of something sacred. But to be unfaithful to that which it stands for makes the wedding ring a disgrace. On one occasion when I was in a motel in another city, I saw a man who was a deacon in a church, sitting at a table, having a very friendly talk with a very beutiful young lady who was not his wife. The thing that impressed me was that as his hand hung over the side of the table, the light was shining on his wedding ring, making it stand out. I thought, what a mockery! When the man saw me, he was embarrassed, of course. But, you see, the wedding ring was meaningless.

The point Paul is making here is that circumcision should stand for something.

> **But he is a Jew, which is one inwardly; and circumcision is that of the heart, in the spirit, and not in the letter; whose praise is not of men, but of God [Rom. 2:29].**

The Mosaic Law had already stated that circimcision was of the heart. Listen to Moses in Deuteronomy 10:16: "Circumcise therefore the foreskin of your heart, and be no more stiff-necked."

# CHAPTER 3

*THEME: Availability of a righteousness from God*

**What advantage then hath the Jew? or what profit is there of circumcision? [Rom. 3:1].**

"**P**rofit" means that which is surplus, that which is excess, and the question has to do with the outward badge of God's special covenant with the Jews, circumcision.

It looks as if Paul is in danger of erasing a distinction which God has made. The question is, if Jew and Gentile are on the same footing before God, what then is the supposed advantage of the Jew and what good is circumcision?

Let me give you a statement of Dr. James Stifler: "If circumcision in itself does not give righteousness, if uncircumcision does not preclude it, what profit was there ever in it? A distinction that God made among men seems, after all, not to be one." Now, this is the same question, I think, that we hear today. I get it because the gospel that I preach says that church membership has no advantage for salvation, that any rite or ritual you go through is meaningless as far as salvation is concerned. God has the world shut up to a Cross. He's not asking you to join anything or do anything. What God is asking the lost sinner to do is to believe on the Lord Jesus Christ, and he shall be saved. And until a person answers that question, then God hasn't anything else to say to him. After he's saved, then God probably will talk to him about church membership and about baptism. We hear people say today, "Well, doesn't my church, my creed, my membership, my baptism help toward my salvation?" The answer is no, it doesn't help you toward salvation. But if you are saved, then these things are a badge, and these things are a means of communicating to the world who you are. But if you're not measuring up, then your church membership and your baptism are a disgrace; and instead of being sacred they become profane.

Now Paul is going to answer the question: What advantage then did the Jews have?

**Much every way: chiefly, because that unto them were committed the oracles of God [Rom. 3:2].**

Paul is saying, "Yes, the Jew has an advantage." The advantage, however, created a responsibility. We need to note carefully the advantage the Jew had because there is a great deal of confusion in this area. I know men who are teaching in theological seminaries who make no distinction between Judaism in the Old Testament and the church in the New Testament. Paul is making it clear that God not only gave to the nation Israel the oracles of God—they were the ones who communicated the Word of God—but in the Word of God was something special for them. God is not through with the nation Israel. I always test a theologian at that particular point: Does God have a future for Israel? My friend, if God doesn't have a future for Israel, I don't think He has a future for you either or for that theological professor. All God's promises are in the same Word of God. God is going to make good John 3:16, and God is also going to make good His covenant with Abraham in chapter 12 of Genesis. Listen again to Dr. Stifler as he is speaking of Israel: "His advantage was not that God sowed Judaism and the world reaped Christianity. That blots out Judaism. It was first of all 'that unto them were committed to the oracles of God,' not that they were made a mere Bible depository, but that God gave them, as Jews, promises, not yet fulfilled, and peculiarly their own. The Old Testament, the record of its oracles, contains not one promise either of or to the church as an organization. It does not predict a church; it foreshadows a kingdom in which the Jew shall be head and not lose his national distinction as he does in the church." Now, friend, I think that's one of the most important and profound statements that has been made concerning the Word of God. At this point "great" theologians differ. Dr. Adolph Saphir was a converted Jew, and he made this tremendous, pointed statement: "The view that is so prevalent, that Israel is a shadow of the church, and now that the type is fulfilled vanishes from our horizon, is altogether unscriptural. Israel is not the shadow fulfilled and absorbed *in the church,* but the *basis* on which the church rests." Friend, that is an important comment, and that's what Paul is saying here—that the Jew has a great advantage. God has a future for him, and his faithlessness will not destroy God's promise. Listen to Paul:

> **For what if some did not believe? shall their unbelief make the faith of God without effect? [Rom. 3:3].**

"If some were without faith" is a better translation. Shall their lack of faith cancel out the faithfulness of God? This is another objection that would be put up, and Paul meets this by going back to the first. Now if the advantage of the Jew did not serve the intended purpose, does this not mean God's faithfulness to His people is annulled? The Jew failed; doesn't that mean God failed? No. God's promise to send Israel the Redeemer was not defeated by their willful disobedience and rejection. All His promises for the future of the nation will be fulfilled to His glory in spite of their unbelief. Now, my friend, you may not like that, but I personally thank God that His promises to me do not depend on my faithfulness. If it had depended on me, I would have been lost long ago. Thank God for *His* faithfulness!

> **God forbid: yea, let God be true, but every man a liar; as it is written, That thou mightest be justified in thy sayings, and mightest overcome when thou art judged [Rom. 3:4].**

In other words, the unbeliever that raises this question is a liar and God is going to make him out to be a liar someday. Why? Because the faithfulness of God is true and cannot be changed. How important that is! John says, "He that believeth on the Son of God hath the witness in himself: he that believeth not God hath made him a liar; because he believeth not the record that God gave of his Son" (1 John 5:10). How bad is it not to believe that God gave His Son to die for you? Well, I'll tell you how bad it is: You make God a liar. That's what you do when you reject His Son.

> **But if our unrighteousness commend the righteousness of God, what shall we say? Is God unrighteous who taketh vengeance? (I speak as a man) [Rom. 3:5].**

By some subtle sophistry it might be argued that since the nation's unbelief merely puts in contrast the faithfulness of God, God is not just to punish that which brings greater glory to Himself. A better translation would be: "Is God unjust who visiteth with wrath by judging" these people? Now this is the severest criticism that Paul faced in preaching the gospel of the grace of God. If God uses sin to get glory to Himself, then He should not punish the sinner. This, of course, was used by some as an excuse for sinning. We'll find this again in Romans 6:1 and will deal with it then. Paul asks the question in such a way in the Greek as to demand a negative answer. God is not unjust. He says, "I speak as a man." That doesn't mean that Paul is not writing this particular passage by inspiration, but rather that he is presenting this question from the finite and human standpoint.

Now, the whole point is this: if my unrighteousness reveals the marvelous, wonderfully infinite faithfulness of God in the grace of God, then has God a right to judge me? That's what Paul is asking here. This makes it very clear that the unsaved world in Paul's day understood that Paul was preaching salvation by the grace of God. How wonderful!

> **God forbid: for then how shall God judge the world? [Rom. 3:6].**

If God would have no right to judge us because our sin merely reveals the grace of God, then God would have no right to judge any person, you see, because they would reveal something of the common grace of God.

Paul's answer is again an emphatic and categorical denial of any such premise that God is unjust. The argument here is that if this particular sin merely enhances the glory of God and the grace of God, then all sin would do the same. Therefore, God would not be able to judge the world. He would abdicate His throne as Judge of all the earth. This specious argument would say that Hitler ought not to be judged. And whoever you are—even if you are an unbeliever—you *do* believe that some people ought to be judged. Now, you may not think that *you* ought to be, but you believe *somebody* ought to be judged. Everyone believes that. We have that innate sense within us today, and God has put it there.

> **For if the truth of God hath more abounded through my lie unto his glory; why yet am I also judged as a sinner? [Rom. 3:7].**

The lie here means moral falsehood. Each individual could claim exemption from the judgment of God because his sin had advanced the glory of God.

> **And not rather, (as we be slanderously reported, and as some affirm that we say,) Let us do evil, that good may come? whose damnation is just [Rom. 3:8].**

In this verse Paul drives his argument to its logical, yet untenable conclusion. This is called an *argumentum ad absurdum*. If sin magnifies the glory of God, then the more sin the more glory. Some had falsely accused Paul of teaching this absurdity. It was ridiculous, for it was Paul who insisted that God must judge sin. As surely as there is sin there must be judgment. You see, this facetious type of argument which Paul has met here makes a Robespierre a saint in the name of utilitarianism. It's the old bromide that the end justifies the means.

Now we come to this section where we have the accusation of "guilty" by God against mankind. Paul is going to conclude this section on sin by bringing mankind up before the Judge of all the earth. And the accusation of "guilty" is made by God against all mankind— both Jew and Gentile, black and white, male and female, rich and poor. It doesn't make any difference who we are; if we belong to the human race, you and I stand guilty before God. And then Paul is going to take us to God's clinic. It's a real spiritual clinic, and the Great Physician is going to look at us. We see that there are fourteen different charges made; six of them before the Judge and the other eight before the Great Physician who says we're sick. In fact, we're sick nigh unto death. To tell the truth, we are dead in trespasses and sin. That is our condition.

> **What then? are we better than they? No, in no wise: for we have before proved both Jews and Gentiles, that they are all under sin [Rom. 3:9].**

Now Paul doesn't mean "proved" here. That word is a little too strong; it does not have quite that shade of meaning, because Paul is not trying to prove man a sinner. Rather, he is showing that God judges sin. He assumes man is a sinner, and you don't have to assume it—it is evident. He is merely stating that which is very obvious today. The better word is *charged*—"for we have before *charged* both Jews and Gentiles, that they are all under sin." He is just stating the case, by the way, that it doesn't make any difference who we are today—high or low, rich or poor, good or bad—we're all under sin.

Now it's very important to understand what it means to be "under sin." Man is a sinner four different ways. God is giving man four strikes (in baseball you get only three). (1) Man is a sinner by act. (2) Man is a sinner by nature. Sinning does not make a sinner; we sin because we are sinners. (3) Man is a sinner by imputation. We'll see that later in this epistle. (4) The estate of man is under sin. We all are under sin—the entire human family.

This is the first charge:

> **As it is written, There is none righteous, no, not one [Rom. 3:10].**

This should read, "It is written *that* there is none righteous, no, not one," because it is a free rendering of Psalm 14:1.

He makes the positive statement that "none . . . doeth good." "Doeth good" and righteousness are the same. What does it mean to be righteous? Well, it means to be right. Right with whom? We are to be right with God. And if we are going to be right with God, it is a little different from being right with your fellow man. When we have differences with friends, we may or may not be to blame, but we have to reach some sort of compromise. But if we are going to be right with God, we are going to play according to His rules. Actually, you can't play games with Him. You see, God's salvation is a take it or leave it proposition. God is not forcing anybody to take His salvation. You don't have to be saved. You can turn it down. God says, "This is My universe. You're living on My little world, using My sunshine and My water and My air, and I have worked out a plan of salvation that is true to My character and My nature. My plan and My program is the one that's going to be carried out. You're a sinner, and I want to save you because I love you. Now here it is. Take it or leave it." That's what God is saying to a lost world. This is what He is saying to you. Have you accepted it? Well, I want you to know that I have accepted it. To be right with God, then, means to accept His salvation.

When I was in school, I had a professor of sociology who really enjoyed batting that little ball around, saying, "Who is right? Who is going to make the rules?" Well, I know one thing: that professor is not going to make the rules. I know something else: I am not going to make the rules, and you are not going to make the rules either. God makes the rules. Take it or leave it. That is God's plan; that is God's program. There is none who is righteous, none right with God. But He has worked out a plan. No one has done good according to God's standard, according to God's method. That is the Judge's first charge.

The second charge is this:

**There is none that understandeth, there is none that seeketh after God [Rom. 3:11].**

In other words, there is none who acts on the knowledge that he has. No one is the person he would like to be.

The third charge:

"There is none that seeketh after God." God is not concealed today. God is not playing hide-and-seek with man. He has revealed Himself. You remember that Paul told the Athenians, the philosophers on Mars Hill: "And the times of this ignorance God winked at; but now com-

mandeth all men everywhere to repent" (Acts 17:30). He is not wink-
ing at sin today. God is out in the open telling man that he is a sinner
and offering him salvation. And His salvation is clear, you see. That's
what He is saying here. And there is none that seeks after God. The
anthologies of religion say man is out looking for God—how falla-
cious they are! It's claimed that in the evolutionary process religion is
man's search for God. Well, actually, is religion man's search for God?
No. That's not what the Bible teaches. Believe me, man hasn't found
out very much about God on his own. He hasn't advanced very far in
that direction, because he's going the wrong way. He's going away
from God.

Then the fourth charge that He makes is:

**They are all gone out of the way, they are together be-
come unprofitable; there is none that doeth good, no,
not one [Rom. 3:12].**

They've detoured. They left the way they knew was right. And primitive tribes have an ancient tradition that way back at one time their
forefathers knew the living and true God. My friend, if you are honest,
you know that you are not doing what you ought to do. Furthermore,
you are not going to do it, although you know what it is. You have
gone out of the way. Man has deviated from the way. This is the fourth
charge that God makes.

The fifth charge is: "they are together become unprofitable." The
word *unprofitable* suggests overripe, spoiled fruit. It could be translated, "they have altogether become sour." I am very fond of fruit, especially the papaya. But when it passes the ripe state and becomes
rotten, there is nothing quite as bad as that. Mankind is not lush fruit;
he is corrupt fruit. That is what the Judge of all the earth is saying.

The sixth charge: "there is none that doeth good, no, not one."
This is a triple negative. Mankind is like a group of travelers who have
gone in the opposite direction from the right one, and not one can
help the others. Our Lord said to the religious leaders of His day, "You
are blind leaders of the blind" (see Matt. 15:14). That is what the

Judge of all the earth says about you and about me and about everyone
on the face of the earth.

Now Paul transfers us over to God's clinic into the hands of the
Great Physician. This is a spiritual clinic, and the Great Physician
says that we are spiritually sick.

> **Their throat is an open sepulchre; with their tongues
> they have used deceit; the poison of asps is under their
> lips [Rom. 3:13].**

When you go to the doctor, what's the first thing that he says to you?
Well, I have to go in for a regular check-up because of the fact that I
apparently have cancer in my system, and I report regularly in case of
an outbreak. Well, it is a ritual for me to go in, and I sit down in the
little room where he does his examination. Do you know the first
thing that he says to me? "Open your mouth." Then he takes a little
wooden stick and pushes it around in my mouth, and he looks at my
throat. Likewise God, the Lord Jesus, the Great Physician, does that
with mankind. Do you know what He says? "Their throat is an open
sepulchre." Have you ever smelled decaying human flesh? When a
little girl in Nashville was kidnapped many years ago, the sheriff of
the county was a member and a deacon in my church. He called me up
and told me they had found the body of a little girl, and they were
going out to exhume it. He wanted to know if I wanted to go with
them. I got to the place where they had taken the body out—it had
been buried several days—and the body was corrupt. Oh, it was terrible! I've never been as sick in my life as I was at the odor of corrupt
human flesh. I always think of that in connection with this verse.

When God looks down at you, friend, He doesn't say what a sweet,
fine little boy or girl you are. God says you smell like an open grave!
Someone, I think it was Mel Trotter, said, "If we could see ourselves
as God sees us, we couldn't even *stand* ourselves!" Well, that is what
Paul is saying here.

And "with their tongues they have used deceit." That's number
two. And the second thing my doctor says to me (after he looks at my
throat) is, "Stick out your tongue!" That's what the Great Physician

says to the human family. "Stick out your tongue." And when God looks at the tongue of mankind—that means your tongue and mine—do you know what He says? "The poison of asps is under their lips." There's a snake house and a place for reptiles in the zoo in San Diego, California, which I have been through several times. As I look at the vicious fangs of those diamondback rattlers, I think of the poison that is there. Friend, right now, if you go and look in the mirror, you will see a tongue that is far more dangerous than any diamondback rattlesnake. He can't hurt your reputation at all. He can kill your body, but he can't hurt your reputation. You have a tongue that you can use to ruin the reputation of someone else. You can ruin the fair name of some woman. You can ruin the reputation of some man. I think today the most vicious thing in some of our churches is the gossip that is carried on. I actually advised someone not too long ago not to join a certain church, because I happen to know that some of the worst gossips in the world are in that church. And I want to tell you they have slaughtered the reputation of many individuals. Do you know who they are? They are the so-called spiritual crowd. I call them the spiritual snobs, because that's what they are. With their tongues they use deceit, and "the poison of asps [adder's poison] is under their lips." Oh, how vicious the human tongue is! How terrible it can be.

### Whose mouth is full of cursing and bitterness [Rom. 3:14].

This is the fourth thing the Great Physician says about man. His mouth is full of cursing and deceit and fraud; under his tongue is mischief and vanity. Also he is prone to curse. And if you listen to what is being said today, you know that cursing is in the vocabulary of all men, whether he is a ditch digger or a college professor. They're better at using profanity than they are at any other language. A man challenged this verse one time when I was a pastor in downtown Los Angeles. He didn't believe it was true. So I said to him, "Let's test it. You and I will walk out here to the corner, and the first man who comes by, whoever he is, you punch him in the mouth and see what comes out. I guarantee that it will be as God says."

Then God says the fifth thing.

### Their feet are swift to shed blood [Rom. 3:15].

Isaiah 59:7 gives the unabridged version: "Their feet run to evil, and they make haste to shed innocent blood: their thoughts are thoughts of iniquity; wasting and destruction are in their paths." What a picture this is of mankind—"Their feet are swift to shed blood."

### Destruction and misery are in their ways [Rom. 3:16].

Man leaves desolation and distress behind him. This is included in Isaiah 59:7 which we have quoted.

### And the way of peace have they not known [Rom. 3:17].

Man does not know the way of peace. Look about you in the world today. After all these years man is still talking about peace, but he hasn't found it. Just read your newspaper, my friend; there is no peace in this world.

### There is no fear of God before their eyes [Rom. 3:18].

Paul seems to sum up all of man's sin in this final statement. He has no fear of God at all. Man is living as if God does not exist. Man actually defies God. What a picture this gives of mankind!

Now we come to the final thing Paul has to say about sin. Because there are still those who will say, "Well, we have the Law and we'll keep the Law. We will hold onto it."

> **Now we know that what things soever the law saith, it saith to them who are under the law: that every mouth may be stopped, and all the world may become guilty before God [Rom. 3:19].**

Man cannot attain righteousness by the Mosaic Law. It is as if mankind in desperation grabbed for the Law as the proverbial straw when drowning. The Law won't lift him up. Actually, it does the opposite. To hold onto the Law is like a man jumping out of an airplane, and instead of taking a parachute, he takes a sack of cement with him. Well, believe me, the Law will pull you down. It condemns man. It's a ministration of death.

> **Therefore by the deeds of the law there shall no flesh be justified in his sight: for by the law is the knowledge of sin [Rom. 3:20].**

Now, I challenge any person today who believes that you have to keep the Law to be saved to take this verse and explain it. "Therefore by the deeds of the law there shall no flesh be justified in his sight." And "justified" means to be declared righteous, to be saved, to meet God's standards. You can never do it, my beloved. It's absolutely impossible for mankind to do. "By the deeds of the law there shall no flesh be justified." Then what is the purpose of the Law? "By the law is the knowledge of sin." Rather than providing a salvation for man, the Law reveals man to be a sinner.

Between verses 20 and 21 there is a "Grand Canyon" division. We move out of the night into the day. Now Paul begins to speak of God's wonderful salvation. He will talk about justification by faith, which will be explained in the remainder of the chapter.

## AVAILABILITY OF A RIGHTEOUSNESS FROM GOD

> **But now the righteousness of God without the law is manifested, being witnessed by the law and the prophets [Rom. 3:21].**

"The righteousness of God" should be *a* righteousness of God, since the article is absent in the Greek. This "righteousness" is not an attribute of God—He says that He will not share His glory with another—nor is it the righteousness of man. God has already said that ". . . our righteousnesses are as filthy rags . . ." (Isa. 64:6), and God is not taking in dirty laundry. Then what righteousness is Paul speaking of? It is the

righteousness which God provides. Christ has become our righteousness. "But of him are ye in Christ Jesus, who of God is made unto us
wisdom and righteousness, and sanctification, and redemption"
(1 Cor. 1:30). Also we are told in 2 Corinthians 5:21: "For he hath
made him to be sin for us, who knew no sin; that we might be made
the righteousness of God in him." It is very important for us to recognize tht God is the One who provides this righteousness. It's not something that you and I can work out, but rather it is something that God
has provided for us. A righteousness that God demands, God also provides.

This is a righteousness that is apart from the Law, that is, you can't
get it, my friend, by doing something or keeping something—not
even God's Law. You can't keep the Law to begin with. God can't save
you by law for the very simple reason that you can't measure up to it.
God can't accept imperfection, and you and I cannot provide perfection. Therefore, He cannot save us by law. "Being witnessed by the
law and the prophets" means that the Law bore witness to it in that at
the very center of the Mosaic system was a tabernacle where bloody
sacrifices were offered which pointed to Christ. Also the prophets
witnessed to it when they spoke of the coming of Christ, His death
and resurrection. For example, Isaiah prophesied, "All we like sheep
have gone astray; we have turned every one to his own way; and the
LORD hath laid on him the iniquity of us all. . . . Yet it pleased the LORD
to bruise him; he hath put him to grief: when thou shalt make his soul
an offering for sin, he shall see his seed, he shall prolong his days,
and the pleasure of the LORD shall prosper in his hand" (Isa. 53:6, 10).

Both the Law and the prophets witnessed to this righteousness
that God would provide in Christ.

**Even the righteousness of God which is by faith of Jesus
Christ unto all and upon all them that believe: for there
is no difference [Rom. 3:22].**

When I was a young preacher I thought that the grace of God had to go
way down to reach the bad sinners but didn't have to go down so far to
reach others who weren't so bad. But now I know that God's grace has

to go all the way to the bottom to get all of us. Each one of us is completely lost outside of Christ. Either you are absolutely saved in Christ, or you are completely lost outside of Christ. All of us need the righteousness of Christ. There is no difference.

The righteousness of Christ comes to us through our faith in Christ. Great men of the past have given some apt definitions of this righteousness. William Cunningham wrote: "Under law God required righteousness from man. Under grace, He gives righteousness to man. The righteousness of God is that righteousness which God's righteousness requires Him to require." That is a deep definition, but it is a good one. The great Dr. Charles Hodge has given this definition: "That righteousness of which God is the author which is of avail before Him, which meets and secures His approval." Then Dr. Brooks gives this definition: "That righteousness which the Father required, the Son became, and the Holy Spirit convinces of, and faith secures." Dr. Moorehead writes: "The sum total of all that God commands, demands, approves, and Himself provides." I don't believe it can be said any better than the way these men have said it.

Now this righteousness, as we have seen it, is secured by faith, not by works. Let's look at these verses together.

> **Even the righteousness of God which is by faith of Jesus Christ unto all and upon all them that believe: for there is no difference:**

> **For all have sinned, and come short of the glory of God [Rom. 3:22–23].**

Let me give you a free rendering of these verses: Even the righteousness from God which is obtained by faith in Jesus Christ unto all and upon all that believe: for there is no distinction: for all have sinned and fall short of the glory [approval] of God. That this righteousness is by faith, not by works, the Lord Jesus made clear when they asked him, ". . . What shall we do, that we might work the works of God?" Jesus answered and said unto them, "This is the work of God, that ye believe on him whom he hath sent" (John 6:28–29). And the important thing about securing this righteousness of God is not that there's any merit in your faith or that there's merit in just believing. Because, actually, faith is not a work on your part. The *object* of faith is the important thing. Spurgeon put it like this: "It's not thy hope in Christ which saves you. It's Christ. It's not thy joy in Christ that saves you. It is Christ. And it is not thy faith in Christ that saves you, though that be the instrument, it is Christ's blood and merit." Now, friend, that's very important to nail in our thinking.

And that righteousness is like a garment. It is available *to* all, but it only comes *upon* all that believe. And then he says that it's needed by everyone: "For all have sinned, and come short of the glory of God." Now that doesn't mean that there is not a difference in sinners. Let me illustrate this with a very homely illustration. Let's suppose that we folk here in California play a game called "Jumping to Catalina." Catalina Island is out in the Pacific Ocean at least fifteen or twenty miles from the shore of California. We will go down to the pier in Santa Monica, and we will take a big running jump, and we'll see who can jump to Catalina. Somebody's going to say, "That's an impossible jump!" Frankly, no one has jumped it, but it's a lot of fun playing the game. Suppose you and I play the game. You may be able to jump farther than I can jump, but you will miss Catalina. And the fellow who jumps the farthest gets the wettest and has to swim farther back to shore. Of course, nobody could jump to Catalina. Some are better than others, but it's rather childish to play a game like that and say, "I jumped farther than you did. I'm better than you are, and I'm better than half the church members." Suppose you are—and you may well be—but what difference does that make? You have not come up to the glory of God.

**Being justified freely by his grace through the redemption that is in Christ Jesus [Rom. 3:24].**

"Freely" is the Greek word *dōrean*, translated in John 15:25 "without a cause." Our Lord Jesus said that they hated Him freely, without a cause—there was no basis for it. Now Paul is saying, "Being justified freely—without a cause." There is no explanation in us. God doesn't say, "Oh, they are such wonderful people, I'll have to do something for them!" As we have seen before, there is nothing in us that would call out the grace of God, other than our great need. We are justified without a cause. It is by His grace, which means that there is no merit on our part. Grace is unmerited favor; it is love in action.

It is "through the redemption that is in Christ Jesus." Redemption is always connected with the grace of God. The reason that God can save you and me is that Christ redeemed us; He paid a price. He died upon a cross to make it available to us. You see, justification by faith is actually more than subtraction of our sins—that is, forgiveness. It is the addition of the righteousness of Christ. In other words, we are not merely restored to Adam's former position, but now we are placed in Christ where we shall be throughout the endless ages of eternity the sons of God!

John Bunyan was driven almost to distraction because he realized that he was such a great sinner with no righteousness of his own. And he said at that time, "When God showed me John Bunyan as God saw John Bunyan, I no longer confessed I was a sinner, but I confessed that I was sin from the crown of my head to the sole of my feet. I was full of sin." And Bunyan struggled with the problem of how he could stand in God's presence even with his sins forgiven. Where could he gain a standing before God? And so, walking through the cornfields one night, as he wrestled with this problem, the words of Paul (who was another great sinner, who called himself the chief of sinners) came to him, and his burden rolled off his shoulders. The word from Paul was Philippians 3:9: "And be found in him, not having mine own righteousness, which is of the law, but that which is through the faith of Christ, the righteousness which is of God by faith." And when you read Bunyan's *Pilgrim's Progress*, you're reading actually the story of Bunyan's life. And you remember, when Pilgrim came with that great burden on his shoulders through the Slough of Despond, he didn't know what to do until finally he came to the Cross, and there the burden rolled off, and he trusted Christ as his Savior.

"By his grace" is the way God saves us. This is the fountain from which flow down the living waters of God in this age of grace. And so, because of what God has done—sending His Son to die—God is able to save by grace. And Paul in Ephesians 2:4–5 says, "But God, who is rich in mercy [that means He has plenty of it], for his great love where-with he loved us, even when we were dead in sins, hath quickened us together with Christ, (by grace ye are saved;)." And Dr. Newell said of that grace, "The grace of God is infinite love operating by an infinite means—the sacrifice of Christ; and an infinite freedom, unhindered, now, by the temporary restrictions of the law." Today a holy God is free to reach down to meet your needs. How wonderful it is to know a holy God is free to save those who will trust Christ. Dr. Newell again said, "Everything connected with God's salvation is glad in bestowment, infinite in extent, and unchangeable in its character." And it's all available, and only available, in Christ Jesus. He alone could pay the price. As Peter put it to the nation Israel, "Neither is there salvation in any other: for there is none other name under heaven given among men, whereby we must be saved" (Acts 4:12).

> **Whom God hath set forth to be a propitiation through faith in his blood, to declare his righteousness for the remission of sins that are past, through the forbearance of God;**
>
> **To declare, I say, at this time his righteousness: that he might be just, and the justifier of him which believeth in Jesus [Rom. 3:25–26].**

Notice it is "faith in his blood." That blood speaks of His life—". . . without shedding of blood is no remission" (Heb. 9:22). And I tell you, when you put a knife in the body of a man and the blood pours out, that man is a dead man because "the life of the flesh is in the blood." And the life of Jesus Christ was given. That blood is a very precious thing according to Simon Peter.

Now, these two verses are filled with words that are jawbreakers: propitiation, righteousness, remission. Although they are difficult words, don't be too frightened of them, because when we boil them down to our size, we find that in these two verses we have what Calvin called the very marrow of theology. Calvin also wrote: "There is not probably in the whole Bible a passage which sets forth more profoundly the righteousness of God in Christ."

"God hath set forth"—God is the sole architect of salvation, and He is the One today who is able to save. You and I cannot save; no religion can save; no church can save. Paul said to the Corinthians, "And all things are of God, who hath reconciled us to himself by Jesus Christ . . ." (2 Cor. 5:18). He did it. Now, He is giving to us the ministry of reconciliation, and so all that the holy God is asking you and me to do today is to be reconciled to Him. You don't have to do anything to soften God's heart. I have a friend who was an evangelist for years, and he always liked to get people to cry. I used to ask him how many tears you'd have to shed to soften God's heart. "Oh," he said, "don't be ridiculous." I told him, "I'm not being ridiculous. You are. You say you've got to come down to the altar and shed some tears." My friend, God's heart is already soft. All you have to do is come. He is reconciled to you. He says to you, "Be ye reconciled to God." Christ has been "set forth"; that is, He has been exhibited or displayed.

"To be a propitiation" points back to the time over nineteen hundred years ago when Christ was set forth as the Savior. You will recall that the veil of the temple hid the mercy seat and only the high priest could go in past that veil. But today Christ has been set before us as the mercy seat. Speaking of the mercy seat, the writer of Hebrews says, "And over it the cherubims of glory shadowing the mercy-seat . . ." (Heb. 9:5)—the Greek word for mercy seat, hilasterion, is the same word translated "propitiation." Christ has been set forth as the mercy seat. You recall that the poor publican cried out, because he needed a mercy seat, ". . . God be merciful to me a sinner" (Luke 18:13), which literally is, "God, if there were only a mercy seat for me, a poor publican, to come to!" You see, when a Jew became a publican, he cut himself off from the temple and from the mercy seat that was there. Paul is saying that now there is on display a mercy seat— God hath set forth Christ to be a propitiation through faith in His blood. It is wonderful to know that we have a holy God who in joy and in satisfaction and delight can hold out to the world today a mercy seat.

And God doesn't reluctantly save you. If you come, He saves you wholeheartedly, abundantly. Some folk tell me that after I am saved I still have to search and pray and tarry for something more. My friend, when I came to Jesus, I got *everything* (see Eph. 1:3). Oh, how good He was! He didn't hold back anything. And He says to come, He can accept you. ". . . him that cometh to me I will in no wise cast out" (John 6:37). Actually, you and I were shut out from a holy God. But the way now has been opened up for us by His blood.

"To declare his righteousness for the remission of sins are past." That doesn't mean your sins and my sins of the past; it means the sins of those who lived before the Cross. You see, back in the Old Testament, they brought a little lamb. And I'm sure you don't take a little lamb to church to sacrifice. Today it would be sinful to do that. But back then, before Christ came, it was required; the Law required it. Now, that little lamb pointed to the coming of Christ. No one back in those days believed that the little lamb could take away sins. I don't think any of them did. Suppose you had been there when Abel brought a little lamb to God, "Abel, do you think this little lamb is going to take away your sin?" He would have told you no. And you would have said, "Then why did you bring it?" His answer would have been, "God required it. God commanded us to bring it." Hebrews 11:4 tells us "By faith Abel offered unto God a more excellent sacrifice than Cain. . . ." In other words, he did it by revelation, because "faith cometh by hearing, and hearing by the word of God" (Rom. 10:17). The only way Abel could have brought that sacrifice by faith was for God to have told him to bring it. And that is what God did.

You might have said to Abel, "Specifically what do you think God has in mind?" And I think he would have said this, "Well, God has told my mother that there's coming a Savior. We don't know when, but until He comes, we're to do this because we're to come by faith." And so the "sins that are past" means that up to the time when Christ died, God saved on *credit*. God did not save Abraham because he brought a sacrifice. God never saved any of them because they brought a sacrifice. A sacrifice pointed to Christ. When Christ came, He paid for *all* the sins of the past and also for the sins this side of the Cross.

"To declare, I say, at this time his righteousness: that he might be just, and the justifier of him which believeth in Jesus." On this side of the Cross we don't bring a sacrifice, but we are to trust in Christ and His blood.

Now Paul raises a question:

**Where is boasting then? It is excluded. By what law? of works? Nay: but by the law of faith [Rom. 3:27].**

If God is saving by faith in Christ and not by your merit, your works, then where is boasting? What is it that you and I have to crow about? We can't even boast of the fact that we're fundamental in doctrine. We have nothing to glory in today. Paul asks, "Where is boasting then?" And he answers the question he raises.

"It is excluded. By what law? of works? Nay: but by the law of faith." The word *law* in the first instance is not restricted to the Old Testament Law but means the *principle* of law—any law, anything that you think you can do. The second reference to *law* excludes the Old Testament Law and means simply a rule or principle of faith. In other words, God has the human race not on the merit system, but on the basis of simply believing what He has done for us. Therefore, it excludes boasting.

**Therefore we conclude that a man is justified by faith without the deeds of the law [Rom. 3:28].**

This is not a conclusion that Paul is coming to or even a summing up of what he has said. Rather, he is giving an explanation of why boasting is excluded. Why is boasting excluded? Man is justified by faith.

Now Paul not only drives the nail in, he turns the board over and clinches it. Listen to him:

**Is he the God of the Jews only? is he not also of the Gentiles? Yes, of the Gentiles also [Rom. 3:29].**

In other words, does God belong to the Jews alone and not also to the Gentiles? And Paul says, "Yes, to the Gentiles also." Now, listen to this. This is a very cogent argument. Paul says, "If justification is by the law, then God *does* belong to the Jews. But if justification is by faith, then He is the God of both Jews and Gentiles." Now, notice the logic of this. If the Jew persisted in this position, then there must be two Gods—one for the Jews, one for the Gentiles. But the Jew would not allow this. He was a monotheist, that is, he believed in one God. Probably the greatest statement that ever was given to the nation Israel was Deuteronomy 6:4, "Hear, O Israel: Jehovah, our Elohim is one Jehovah" (literal translation mine). That was the clarion message He gave in the pagan world before Christ came.

> **Seeing it is one God, which shall justify the circumci-**
> **sion by faith, and uncircumcision through faith [Rom.**
> **3:30].**

In other words, there's only one God. And in the Old Testament, He gave man the Law. Man failed. God didn't save them by their keeping the Law; salvation was always by the sacrifice which man brought in faith, pointing to the coming of the Lord Jesus Christ.

> **Do we then make void the law through faith? God for-**
> **bid: yea, we establish the law [Rom. 3:31].**

The reference to the Law, I think, brings in another meaning of this word. It is not restricted to the Mosaic system here. Neither does it refer to just any law. Rather, it refers to the entire Old Testament revelation. "Faith" excluded the works of the Law. But did it abrogate the entire Old Testament revelation? Of course not! Paul will demonstrate in the next chapter by Old Testament illustrations of two men, Abraham and David, that it did not exclude that. These two key men, outstanding men, were saved, not by law but by faith. To begin with, Abraham was born and lived and died four hundred years before the Law was ever given. Abraham did not live on the basis of the Mosaic Law since it was not yet given in his day. God saved him on a different basis, which is *by faith.* And somebody says, "Well, then what about David?" Now, very honestly, do you think David could have been saved by keeping the Law? Of course he couldn't. The Old Testament made it very clear that David *broke* the Law. And yet God saved him. How? Well, He saved him by faith. David trusted God and believed

God. Even in his sin, he came in confession to God. God accepted him and saved him by faith.

Today, my friend, when you and I will take the position that we're sinners and come to God and trust Christ as our Savior—regardless of who we are, where we are, how we are or when we are—God will save us. For God today has put man on one basis and one basis alone. His question is, What will you do with My Son who died for you on the Cross?

# CHAPTER 4

*THEME: Abraham; David· Abraham justified by faith*

In this great section of justification by faith, we have seen the doctrine. Paul has vividly stated that man is a sinner. Then he revealed that God provides a righteousness for sinners, and justification by faith has been explained. Now he will illustrate this truth with two men out of the Old Testament: Abraham and David.

In Paul's day Abraham and David were probably held in higher esteem by the nation Israel than any other two whose lives are recorded in the Old Testament. Abraham was the founder of the Hebrew race, and David was their greatest king. Paul uses these two Old Testament worthies as illustrations to establish his statement in chapter 3 that there is concord and agreement between the Law and the gospel. Although they represent two diametrically opposed systems, neither contradicts nor conflicts with the other. And they are not mutually exclusive. Even under the Law and before the Law, faith was God's sole requirement. Abraham, before the Law, was justified by faith. And David, under the Law, sang of justification by faith. Paul is not presenting some strange new doctrine which cancels out the Old Testament and leaves the Jew afloat on the sea of life holding onto an anchor rather than being in a lifeboat. Paul is showing that Abraham and David are in the same lifeboat, which he is offering his own people in his day, labeled "justification by faith." The Law was a pedagogue—it took the man under Law by the hand to lead him to the Lord Jesus Christ.

## ABRAHAM

Now we see in the first five verses that Abraham was justified by faith.

> **What shall we say then that Abraham our father, as pertaining to the flesh, hath found? [Rom. 4:1].**

Let's rearrange the modifiers and phrases to help us follow the thought of Paul: Therefore, what shall we say that Abraham, our first father, has found according to the flesh, that is, by natural human effort? The *therefore* that opens this chapter connects this argument with what Paul has been talking about back in the third chapter. The gospel excludes boasting and establishes the Law, as we have seen. Abraham and David confirm Paul in this thesis.

Paul uses the idiomatic phrase "What shall we say?" here and in the other argumentative portions of this epistle. In the first division, Paul did not attempt to prove or argue that man is a sinner. For this reason we did not find this phrase there. Also in the last section of this epistle, which is practical, it is entirely omitted.

"Abraham, our first father" reveals that the nation Israel began with Abraham. "First father," I think, is a peculiar expression. It reveals the importance attached to Abraham, who was first chronologically and also first in importance. Many years ago when I was a pastor in Nashville, several friends that I had known before I studied for the ministry—they were Jewish friends—invited me to come up one evening to speak to a group in the Young Men's Hebrew Association. So I spoke to them on the glories of the Mosaic Law. I was amazed to find that they reckoned their ancestry from Abraham—they never went past Abraham. Quite a few of their questions revealed that, and finally I asked them some questions. I asked, "Don't you count Noah or Adam in the line?" These young Jewish friends laughed and said, "No, we stop with Abraham. He's our first father."

"Pertaining to the flesh" could modify *Abraham,* or it could modify the verb *has found.* What has he found according to the flesh? Abraham has found that Abraham's works according to the flesh did not produce boasting but produced shame and confusion. That was Abraham's works. He had nothing to boast of. Oh, don't misunderstand; I think Abraham was a great man, and especially in that matter of Lot. He wouldn't let the kings of Sodom and Gomorrah reward him. But in another section Abraham didn't believe God, and he ran down to Egypt. This matter of that little Egyptian maid that he got and the son that came from her, these are things that are not to be boasted of by Abraham.

Now notice how Paul develops this.

**For if Abraham were justified by works, he hath whereof
to glory; but not before God [Rom. 4:2].**

If Abraham were justified (declared to be righteous) by works—that is,
the works of the flesh "he hath whereof to glory," but not before God.
He can glory in self, but he cannot glory before God. It was assumed
that Abraham had good works that counted before God. And the fact
of the matter is that Abraham had many good works. But the startling
thing was to discover that these good works were not the ground of
salvation but were the result of his salvation and the result of being
justified by faith. You see, James and Paul did not contradict each
other when James said, "Was not Abraham our father justified by
works, when he had offered Isaac his son upon the altar? (James 2:21).
The works that James described are not the works of the flesh under
the Law, because Abraham wasn't under the Law. They were works of
faith. Abraham believed God, and he offered up Isaac. But did he actually do it? No, God stopped him and would not let him go through
with it. Why? Because it was wrong. You see, Paul and James quote
the same verse: Abraham believed God, and He counted it unto him
for righteousness (cf. Gen. 15:6; James 2:23; Rom. 4:3). But James
goes to the end of Abraham's life, to the time that he offered up Isaac.
Abraham stood on the same ground on which the weakest sinner
stands. Granted that he did have works in which to boast, but he could
never boast before God, because God does not accept the works of the
flesh. The works of the flesh cannot stand before His holiness, and
certainly Abraham's works were tinctured.

**For what saith the scripture? Abraham believed God,
and it was counted unto him for righteousness [Rom.
4:3].**

Paul appeals to the Scripture as final authority. He even personifies
it here—the Scripture is God speaking. What does the Scripture
say? There is no other authority to which he can appeal. It was
Dr. Benjamin Warfield who made this statement: "The Bible is the

Word of God in such a way that whatever the Bible says *God* says."

How I wish that more men who claim to be evangelical really believed the Word of God—that it *is* the Word of God, that it is God speaking. Paul quotes from the Old Testament directly about sixty times in this epistle. This quotation is, of course, from Genesis 15:6: "And he believed in the LORD; and he counted it to him for righteousness." Paul is saying, "Hear what the Scripture says; God is speaking to you in His Word." How tremendous this is.

This promise was given to Abraham at a time when he raised a question with God: ". . . what wilt thou give me, seeing I go childless . . . ?" (Gen. 15:2). God gave him no assurance other than a confirmation of the promise that his seed would be like the stars. In other words, Abraham simply believed God. He took the naked Word of God at face value, and he rested in it. Newell puts it like this: "There was no honor, no merit, in Abraham believing the faithful God, who cannot lie. The honor was God's. When Abraham believed God, he did the one thing that a man can do without doing anything! God made the statement, the promise, and God undertook to fulfill it. Abraham believed in his heart that God told the truth. There was no effort here. Abraham's faith was not an act, but an attitude. His heart was turned completely away from himself to God and His promise. This left God free to fulfill that promise. Faith was neither a meritorious act by Abraham, nor a change of character or nature in Abraham; he simply believed God would accomplish what He had promised: 'In thee shall all the families of the earth be blessed' (Gen. 12:3)." How wonderful!

"Counted unto him for righteousness." God counted, reckoned, it to him. God put it to Abraham's account. He imputed it over to him for righteousness. It was not righteousness, but that is how God reckoned it.

> **Now to him that worketh is the reward not reckoned of grace, but of debt.**
>
> **But to him that worketh not, but believeth on him that justifieth the ungodly, his faith is counted for righteousness [Rom. 4:4–5].**

It is a general rule that a workman is paid wages for the services that he renders. A man works for so much an hour, or he is paid so much for a particular job. Obviously Abraham was not a workman, for he did not earn what he received. His salvation was received on the only other basis, and that was undeserved favor—by the grace of God—and he believed God. "But to him that worketh not" that is, there is nothing that you can do that will merit salvation. But you believe on Him, that is, on God, who declares the ungodly righteous. And the only kind of people God is saving are unrighteous people. Somebody says, "You mean that He doesn't save good people?" Well, do you want to name one? God will save any man who is good. But Scripture, as we've already seen, says, "There is none righteous, no, not one" (Rom. 3:10). This is according to God's standard, not according to my little standard or your standard. If you want to name somebody who is good, you will make God out a liar. Are you prepared to do that? And, of course, you would have to prove your point.

"His faith is counted for righteousness." Faith is the only condition. God accepts faith in lieu of works. There is no merit in faith, but it is the only way of receiving that which God freely offers. Faith honors God and secures righteousness for man. God put down righteousness in Abraham's account to his credit. His faith counted for what it was not—a righteousness from God. This is important to see.

## DAVID

**Even as David also describeth the blessedness of the man, unto whom God imputeth righteousness without works [Rom. 4:6].**

David lived under the Law—Abraham did not because no law had been given during his lifetime. The Mosaic system didn't come along until four hundred years later. However, although David lived under the Law, David could never be saved under the Law. And therefore David described the blessedness that God reckons righteousness without works—because David had no works. The works that he had were evil. And therefore, righteousness must be totally apart and sep-

arate from works. Righteousness must come on an entirely different
principle.

### Saying, Blessed are they whose iniquities are forgiven, and whose sins are covered [Rom. 4:7].

This is a direct quotation from Psalm 32, verses 1 and 2. And this is
one of the great penitential psalms of David—Psalm 51 is the other
one. These verses are the outcome of David's great sin and his confession and acceptance which followed.

"Blessed are they whose iniquities are forgiven." Are you one of
the blessed ones today? Well, I'm glad to be in that company, in that
number. "Blessed" expresses, oh, that glorious, wonderful joy of sins
forgiven! This is the greatest statement of all, and David knew this by
experience.

"Iniquities" is lawlessness. David deliberately broke the law. He
didn't do it ignorantly. He knew what he did, and he was forgiven.

"Are forgiven" refers to a definite and complete act of remission. A
hard-boiled judge may under certain circumstances remit sins. But
this speaks of the tenderness of God by taking the sinner into His arms
of love and receiving him with affection. His sins are covered. How?
Because Jesus Christ died and shed His blood, my friend.

### Blessed is the man to whom the Lord will not impute sin [Rom. 4:8].

In other words, joyful is the man whose sin the Lord will not put to his
account. David was a great sinner. And God put away his sin, as Nathan informed him. Nathan said to David, ". . . The LORD also hath put
away thy sin; thou shalt not die" (2 Sam. 12:13). Nevertheless, David
was chastened. David set his own penalty when he responded to Nathan's account of the rich man who took the poor man's ewe lamb:
"And he shall restore the lamb fourfold . . ." (2 Sam. 12:6). Four of
David's children were killed—the child of Bathsheba, Amnon his
firstborn, Absalom, and Adonijah. Sorrow plagued David all the days
of his life. David's guilt was not put on his account, though—another

bore it for him. Little wonder that he could say, "Joyful is the man whose sin the Lord will in no wise put to his account."

## ABRAHAM JUSTIFIED BY FAITH

**Cometh this blessedness then upon the circumcision only, or upon the uncircumcision also? for we say that faith was reckoned to Abraham for righteousness [Rom. 4:9].**

The argument now returns to Abraham to illustrate that justification is universal. Since David has spoken of the joy of the man under law who has been forgiven, the answer of the Jew would be that David belonged to the circumcision and only the circumcision could expect this joy. For this reason Paul returns to Abraham to show that Abraham was justified before the Law was given and also before he was circumcised.

**How was it then reckoned? when he was in circumcision, or in uncircumcision? Not in circumcision, but in uncircumcision [Rom. 4:10].**

God made the promise to him, and he believed God long before there was any kind of agreement made at all—other than that God said He would do it. Abraham believed the naked Word of God.

**And he received the sign of circumcision, a seal of the righteousness of the faith which he had yet being uncircumcised: that he might be the father of all them that believe, though they be not circumcised; that righteousness might be imputed unto them also:**

**And the father of circumcision to them who are not of the circumcision only, but who also walk in the steps of that faith of our father Abraham, which he had being yet uncircumcised.**

> For the promise, that he should be the heir of the world,
> was not to Abraham, or to his seed, through the law, but
> through the righteousness of faith [Rom. 4:11–13].

God made that promise to Abraham long before circumcision was introduced. Abraham just believed God; that's all.

> For if they which are of the law be heirs, faith is made
> void, and the promise made of none effect:
>
> Because the law worketh wrath: for where no law is,
> there is no transgression.
>
> Therefore it is of faith, that it might be by grace [Rom.
> 4:14–16a].

You see, God saved Abraham by faith alone.

Now notice something else here. Abraham was justified actually by faith in the resurrection.

> And being not weak in faith, he considered not his own
> body now dead, when he was about an hundred years
> old, neither yet the deadness of Sarah's womb [Rom.
> 4:19].

There is no merit in faith itself. You see, there was nothing around Abraham in which he could trust—nothing that he could feel, nothing that he could see, *nothing.* All he did was believe God. That's important.

> He staggered not at the promise of God through unbelief; but was strong in faith, giving glory to God [Rom.
> 4:20].

He was not double-minded. That's the whole thought here. He looked away from his circumstances to the promise. He believed the promise, in spite of the fact that the circumstances nullified it. He put confi-

dence in the promise because of the One who gave it, thus giving
worship to God. You see, man was created to glorify God, but by disobedience he did the opposite. And, my friend, the only way you can
glorify God is to believe Him.

> **And being fully persuaded that, what he had promised,
> he was able also to perform [Rom. 4:21].**

"Fully persuaded" means that he was filled brimful. There was no
room for doubt.

> **And therefore it was imputed to him for righteousness
> [Rom. 4:22].**

This faith in the resurrection—life from the dead—is what God accepted from Abraham in lieu of his own righteousness, which he did
not have. God declared Abraham righteous for his faith in the promise
of God to raise up a son out of the tomb of death, that is, the womb of
Sarah. God promises eternal life to those who believe that He raised
up His own Son from the tomb of Joseph of Arimathaea, the place of
death.

> **Now it was not written for his sake alone, that it was
> imputed to him;**

> **But for us also, to whom it shall be imputed, if we be-
> lieve on him that raised up Jesus our Lord from the dead
> [Rom. 4:23–24].**

The womb of Sarah was a tomb. It was a place of death. But out of that
came life. Abraham believed God. And this is what the Lord Jesus
meant when He said, "Your father Abraham rejoiced to see my day:
and he saw it, and was glad" (John 8:56).

> **Who was delivered for our offences, and was raised
> again for our justification [Rom. 4:25].**

That is faith, not only in the death of Christ, but also in His resurrection. Matthew Henry put it like this: "In Christ's death He paid our debt; in His resurrection He took out our acquittance." God justifies those who believe in the death and resurrection of Christ. How wonderful this is! Have you gone that far with God? Do you believe Him?

# CHAPTER 5

*THEME:* *Benefits of salvation; sanctification of the saint*

As we come to the fifth chapter of Romans, we find Paul answering one of the questions that would naturally arise in the minds of those who had read his epistle to this point. He has told us that we have been saved by the redemption that we have in Christ, the redemption that had been purchased at tremendous price upon the Cross. It delivers us from the guilt of sin so that the sin question has been settled. This means that we will not come before God for judgment which will determine our salvation. It means that an eternal home is waiting for those who have trusted Christ. Now the question Paul will answer is: What about the here and now?

I have heard liberal preachers say, "I do not believe in a religion of the hereafter; I believe in a religion of the here and now." In San Francisco in the early days of the "hippie" movement, I was talking to a young vagrant on a street corner, and he didn't want to hear about Christianity. He said, "That's 'pie in the sky by and by' religion, and I don't care for that." And so I said to this young fellow, "Then you believe in getting your pie here and now and not by and by?" He said, "That's right." I told him that it didn't look to me like he was getting very much pie in the here and now, and he admitted that he wasn't. So I said, "Well, it is tragic indeed to miss the pie here and now, and miss it hereafter also."

Paul now is going to show that there are certain benefits that accrue to the believer right here and now when he trusts Christ, when he's been justified by faith in the redemption that we have in Christ. And actually these are benefits that the world is very much concerned about, and would like to have them.

Many people are spending a great deal of money today trying to attain the things that are the present benefits of every believer. That doesn't mean that all believers are enjoying them. However, God has them on the table for you, and all you have to do is reach over and take them (see Eph. 1:3).

## BENEFITS OF SALVATION

1. Peace

> **Therefore being justified by faith, we have peace with God through our Lord Jesus Christ [Rom. 5:1].**

"Therefore being justified by faith" refers to the one act of faith the moment we trust Christ.

"We have peace with God through our Lord Jesus Christ."

The Bible mentions several kinds of peace. First, there's world peace. The United Nations has worked for it as the old League of Nations did. They didn't get anywhere in the past, and they're not getting anywhere today. As I write this, a great many people believe that if you protest loudly enough you can bring peace to the world by human manipulation or psychological gyrations. Well, my friend, as long as there is sin in the hearts of men, there never will be peace in the world—not until the Prince of Peace comes. Christ will bring peace on this earth. But world peace is not the kind of peace that Paul is talking about here.

Then there is that peace which is known as tranquility of soul. That is the peace to which the Lord Jesus referred when He said to His disciples, "Peace I leave with you, my peace I give unto you: not as the world giveth, give I unto you . . ." (John 14:27). This is a peace that comes to certain believers who have trusted Christ and who are resting in Him and who are doing His will. I wish I could say that I experience this peace all the time. I do not. I recognize that it is available for every believer today. I suppose I am like most believers in that I have up and down experiences. There are times when this peace floods my soul, and it is wonderful. But there are times when I am under pressure or under tension or when I am weary and this peace somehow eludes me. However, Paul is not referring to the peace of personal tranquility.

Then there is a third kind of peace which Paul mentions to the Philippian believers—"the peace that passeth all understanding" (see Phil. 4:7). Well, since it passes all understanding, I certainly don't know what it is, and I have a notion that you don't know either.

The peace Paul is talking about, which he lists as the first benefit of salvation, is "peace *with God* through our Lord Jesus Christ." This is the peace that comes to the soul of one who has trusted Christ as Savior and knows that God no longer has any charge against him, that he is no longer guilty. He knows that God, who had to be against him in the past, is now *for* him. He knows that he has a salvation that is permanent and eternal. This is the peace that comes because of sins forgiven and because everything is right between you and God. You will notice that Paul mentions again and again that we have peace through the blood of Jesus Christ, which means that everything is all right between our soul and God. That is wonderful peace!

This was explained to me by a wonderful pastor when I was a young boy in my teens. He said that when man sinned in the Garden of Eden, not only did man run away from God—and found himself alienated from the life of God, with no capacity for God and no inclination to turn to Him—but God also had to turn away from man. Then when Christ died on the Cross, God turned around, so that now a holy God can say to a lost sinner, "Come." His arms are outstretched. He says, "Come unto me, all ye that labour and are heavy laden, and I will rest you" (Matt. 11:28, literal translation mine). This is peace, the rest of redemption.

My friend, God is reconciled. You don't have to do anything to reconcile Him, as we have seen. A great many people think that you have to shed tears to reconcile God. You don't need tears to soften the heart of God! You don't have to do anything. Because Christ died on the Cross, God is reconciled today. The message of the gospel is, "Be ye reconciled to God." The next move is yours. When you accept His salvation, then you experience peace that your sins have been forgiven.

There are a great many people who pillow their heads at night, not knowing what it is to have peace in their hearts. Oh, how many weary souls today are laboring with a guilt complex and would love to go somewhere to have that guilt removed from their souls! A Christian psychologist told me several years ago, "The only place you can have a guilt complex removed is at the Cross of Christ." Peace is the first wonderful benefit that accrues to the child of God.

## 2. Access

> **By whom also we have access by faith into this grace wherein we stand, and rejoice in hope of the glory of God [Rom. 5:2].**

"Access" means that you and I have access to God in prayer. It's wonderful to have someone to go and talk to about yourself and about your problems and about your friends and your loved ones. Today we as children of God have access to a heavenly Father who will listen to us here and who does answer our prayer. Now, that doesn't mean He answers it the way you want it answered, but He always hears you, and sometimes He shows He is a good heavenly Father by saying no. He will answer according to His wisdom, not according to our will. You will notice that we have access by faith into this grace wherein we stand.

## 3. Hope

"And rejoice in *hope* of the glory of God" is the third benefit. The hope that is mentioned here is the hope that the Scriptures hold out. Paul said to a young preacher by the name of Titus, "Looking for that blessed hope, and the glorious appearing of the great God and our Saviour Jesus Christ" (Titus 2:13). (I don't think looking for the Great Tribulation is very much of a hope. I'm certainly not looking for it because that would be a dread rather than a hope.) To look for the Lord to come and take His church out of this world, that's a glorious hope, and it will take place at His appearing.

Now, the child of God has this hope. That means he has a future. He has something to look forward to. You and I are living in a day when man has all the comforts of life in an affluent society, but the interesting thing is, he has no future. James Reston, one of the reporters and editors of the *New York Times*, several years ago made the statement that in Washington there is a feeling that the problems have so mounted and multiplied that man is totally incapable of solving the problems of this world. The Word of God, you know, goes along with that—I suppose that was one time that the *New York Times* and the Bible agreed. What a dark outlook is being given to us today, and the band can play and you can wave the flag all you want, but you'd better face facts: there's a cancer in the body politic. One of the last statements that Bernard Shaw made before his death was that he had pinned his hopes on atheism, but he had found that atheism did not solve the problems of the world. Then he made this remarkable comment, "You are looking at an atheist who has lost his faith." When an atheist loses his faith, he has nothing in the world to hold on to.

The world today is looking for a hope, looking for a future. This explains the restlessness that is throughout the world, and I think it explains a great many of the movements of the present moment. I believe it has driven a great many folk to alcohol and drug addiction and down other avenues that are dead-end streets. Why? Because they've lost hope of the future.

Well, the child of God has a hope, a blessed hope. And he knows that all things are going to work together for good (see Rom. 8:28). He knows that nothing is going to separate him from the love of God (see Rom. 8:39). How wonderful that hope is, the blessed hope of the church.

4. Triumph in troubles

> **And not only so, but we glory in tribulations also: knowing that tribulation worketh patience;**
>
> **And patience, experience; and experience, hope [Rom. 5:3–4].**

In other words, we *joy* in troubles, knowing that trouble works patience—patience doesn't come automatically—and patience, experience; and experience, hope.

It is quite interesting to see the three words that are associated with trouble. One is joy, another is hope, and the third is patience. God has to work that into us although it is a fruit of the Holy Spirit. In other words, it takes trouble to bring out the best in the believer's life. The only way God can get fruit out of the life of the believer is by pruning the branches. The world does it differently. If you, as an unbeliever, are in a nice, comfortable situation and have no troubles, then you can have fun, you can also be patient, and you may have a little hope as you go along. But that is not the way it is with the child of God. Actually, trouble produces these fruits in our lives.

## 5. Love of God

**And hope maketh not ashamed; because the love of God is shed abroad in our hearts by the Holy Ghost which is given unto us [Rom. 5:5].**

"The love of God is shed abroad in our hearts" doesn't mean our love for God; it means God's love for us. And this love is made real by the Holy Spirit who is given to us.

## 6. The Holy Spirit

This is the first time in the Epistle to the Romans that the ministry of the Holy Spirit is mentioned. This is only a reference to Him in this list of present benefits. We will not come to the ministry of the Holy Spirit until we get to chapter 8 of Romans where He is mentioned more than twenty times. Here we are simply told that the Holy Spirit is given to every believer—not to only some believers, but to all believers. Even to the Corinthians Paul wrote, "What? know ye not that your body is the temple of the Holy Ghost which is in you, which ye have of God, and ye are not your own?" (1 Cor. 6:19). The Corinthian believers were certainly a carnal lot—in fact, Paul called them babes in Christ—yet the Holy Spirit indwelt them. That's wonderful! I'm glad that, when I came to Christ, I got everything God offers in salvation.

And it is the Holy Spirit who actualizes, or makes real, the love of God in the hearts of believers—that is, God's love for us. Today we need to be conscious of the fact that God loves us. How people need to be assured of that in their lives! Only the Spirit of God can make real to us God's love.

Now notice how Paul explains the love of God.

**For when we were yet without strength, in due time Christ died for the ungodly [Rom. 5:6].**

Christ died for the ungodly—not for the good boys and girls, but for ungodly sinners—those who actually were His enemies, who hated Him, to whom He said when they were crucifying Him, ". . . Father, forgive them; for they know not what they do . . ." (Luke 23:34). And, friend, you and I were numbered with the ungodly.

A few years ago I talked to a young man who had *love* written on his cap, on his funny coat, on his trousers, and even on his shoes! I asked him why. He said, "Why, man, God is love." I agreed with that. Then he said, "God saved me by His love." I replied, "I disagree with that. God does not save you by His love."

Now that seems startling to a great many folk even today. But actually, friend, God does not save you by His love. You see, God is more than love; He is holy and He is righteous. God cannot open the back door of heaven and slip sinners in under the cover of darkness, and He can't let down the bars of heaven and bring sinners in. If He does that, He's no better than a crooked judge who lets a criminal off. God has to do something for the guilt of sinners. There must be judgment, you see. However, God does love us. Regardless of who you are or what you have done, God loves you. It is wrong to say to children, "If you are mean, Willie, or if you do what is wrong, God won't love you." The interesting thing is that God will love little Willie, regardless of what he does. And He loves you. You can't keep God from loving you. Now you can get to the place that you do not experience the love of God. For instance, you can't keep the sun from shining, but you can get out of the sunshine. You can put up an umbrella of sin, an umbrella of indifference, an umbrella of stepping out of the will of God, which will keep His love from shining on you. Although all these things will remove you from experiencing God's love, He still loves you.

As I was talking to this young fellow with *love* written on his clothing, I asked him to show me a verse in the Bible that said God saves us by love. Of course he didn't know any. I said, "The Word of God says, 'For by grace are ye saved through faith; and that not of yourselves: it is the gift of God' (Eph. 2:8). God saves us by His grace, not by His love. 'God so loved the world' that He saved the world? Oh, no—He couldn't. A holy God has to be true to His character. But He did this: '. . . God so loved the world, that he gave his only begotten Son, that whosoever believeth in him should not perish, but have everlasting life' (John 3:16)."

God has demonstrated His love for you, my friend, in that He gave His Son to die for you. He paid the penalty for your sin, and our holy God now can save you if you come His way. Of course, you'll have to come *His* way. There is a mistaken idea today that you can come to Him your way. This isn't your universe; it's *His* universe. You and I don't make the rules. *He* makes the rules. And He says that no man comes to Him except through Christ (see John 14:6).

Now notice how he continues.

**For scarcely for a righteous man will one die: yet peradventure for a good man some would even dare to die [Rom. 5:7].**

Do you know any folk who would die for you? Could you put upon the fingers of one hand those who would be willing to die for you? By the way, could you put upon one finger those who love you enough to die for you? Well, you certainly could put it upon one finger, because God loved you enough to send His Son to die for you. And if it were necessary, He would appear today to die for you again, if it would take that to save you. He loves you that much.

**But God commendeth his love toward us, in that, while we were yet sinners, Christ died for us [Rom. 5:8].**

He died for you and me. That is where God revealed His love. And God doesn't save us by love. He now saves us by grace because the guilt of sin has been removed by the death of Christ, and He can hold out His arms and save you today.

## 7. Deliverance from wrath

**Much more then, being now justified by his blood, we shall be saved from wrath through him [Rom. 5:9].**

The "wrath" mentioned here is what the prophets spoke of: "That day is a day of wrath, a day of trouble and distress, a day of wasteness and desolation, a day of darkness and gloominess, a day of clouds and thick darkness" (Zeph. 1:15). What is the great day of wrath? It is what the Lord Jesus called the Great Tribulation. And Paul tells believers that we shall be "saved from wrath." We have been saved from the penalty of sin; He is constantly saving us today from the power of sin; and He is going to save us in the future from the presence of sin. That means that every believer will leave this earth at the Rapture. We will escape that day of wrath, not because we are worthy, but because we have been saved by the grace of God. We have been saved by grace; we live by the grace of God; and ten billion years from today we will still be in heaven by the grace of God. We are saved from wrath through Him—through Christ.

**For if, when we were enemies, we were reconciled to God by the death of his Son, much more, being reconciled, we shall be saved by his life [Rom. 5:10].**

You see, He died down here to save us; He lives up yonder to keep us saved.

## 8. Joy

**And not only so, but we also joy in God through our Lord Jesus Christ, by whom we have now received the atonement [Rom. 5:11].**

We joy in God! I think this is one of the most wonderful statements we have in Scripture. It means that right now, wherever you are, whatever your problems are, my friend, you can joy, rejoice, in God. Just think of it! You can rejoice that He lives and that He is who He is. You can rejoice because He has provided a salvation for us and is willing to save us sinners and bring us into His presence someday. He has worked out a plan to save us because of His love for us. Isn't that enough to make you rejoice? Oh, the child of God should have joy in his heart. He doesn't need to go around smiling like a Cheshire cat, but he certainly ought to have a joyful heart. I love the song, "Let's Just Praise the Lord." These are the eight wonderful benefits of salvation. Let's just praise the Lord!

## SANCTIFICATION OF THE SAINT

We have seen the salvation of the sinner; now we are coming to the sanctification of the saint. In salvation we are declared righteous, but God wants to do more than declare a person righteous. Justification does not *make* a person righteous. It means that before God's holy court, before the bar of heaven, a lost sinner is now declared righteous, but his heart has not been changed. My friend, if you think God intends to leave a sinner in his sin, you are wrong. God wants to make us the kind of folk we should be. So God also has a plan in salvation whereby He not only *declares* a sinner righteous, but He is also going to *make* a sinner righteous. That is, God provides a way that a sinner may grow in grace and become sanctified (set apart) for God.

The remainder of this chapter is labeled potential sanctification. Now let me warn you that you may find this difficult to understand and difficult to accept.

In potential sanctification we have what is known as the federal headship of Adam and Christ.

### HEADSHIP OF ADAM

**Wherefore, as by one man sin entered into the world, and death by sin; and so death passed upon all men, for that all have sinned [Rom. 5:12].**

Let me give you my own translation of this verse, which may bring out the meaning a little better: "On this account (the plan of salvation for all by one Redeemer) just as through one man sin entered (as a principle) into the world, and death through sin, and so death spread throughout upon all men on the ground of the fact that all sinned."

Now we need to understand that the sin we're talking about is the sin of Adam, that first sin of Adam—not his second one or his third one or his fourth one—his first sin of disobedience in the Garden of Eden, which brought death upon all of his offspring.

Now that brings me back to consider something that is very important: You and I are sinners, as we have said, in four different ways. (1) We are sinners because we commit acts of sin. Also, (2) we're sinners by nature (sin doesn't make us sinners, but we sin because we have that nature). (3) We are in the state of sin. God has declared the entire human family under sin. (4) Finally, you and I are also sinners by imputation. That is, Adam acted for the human race because he was the head of it.

It is on the basis of the federal headship of Adam that now God is able through the federal headship of Christ to save those who will trust Christ. This is what theologians have labeled the federal headship. Adam and Christ are representatives of the human race. Adam is the *natural* head of the human race. By the way, I accept that. I saw a bumper sticker that interested me a great deal. It read, "My ancestors were human—sorry about yours." This lays in the dust the idea that you can be a Christian, believing the Word of God, and also accept the theory of evolution. Adam is the head of the human family. That is what Paul is saying here—he is the natural head. And his one act of disobedience plunged his entire offspring into sin. We are all made sinners by Adam's sin.

First, let's see what this does not mean. It does not refer to the fact that we have a sinful nature inherited from Adam. It is true that I got a sinful nature from my father, and he from his father, and on back. Also, I passed on that nature to my child and to my grandchildren. The first grandchild was such a wonderful little fellow, I was beginning to doubt the total depravity of man. But as he began growing up, he began to manifest this depraved nature. Now I have a second grandson, a redheaded boy, and does he have a temper! Now I am convinced again of the total depravity of man. I have seen a manifestation in these two little fellows of a nature they got from their grandmother (I think!). Although you and I do have sinful natures and do pass them on to our offspring, this particular verse does not refer to that fact.

Also, the verse before us that says "all have sinned" does not mean that we are guilty of a sinful act. Of course, we are guilty, but that is not what the verse is talking about.

Now let's see what it does mean. It does refer to the fact that we are so vitally connected with the first father of the human race that before we even had a human nature, before we had committed a sin, even before we were born, we were sinners in Adam.

Maybe you don't like that. But God says that that is the way it is. We see it illustrated in Hebrews 7:9, "And as I may so say, Levi also, who receiveth tithes, payed tithes in Abraham." That is, long before Levi was even born, he paid tithes to Melchisedec. How could he do it? "For he was yet in the loins of his father, when Melchisedec met him" (Heb. 7:10). In just such a way, Adam's sin was imputed to us. What Adam did, we did. God could put all of us in a Garden of Eden and give us the same test He gave to Adam. Do you think you would do any better with your sinful nature than Adam did without a sinful nature? I don't think so. We might as well accept the fact that Adam's one act of disobedience made all of us sinners.

Now let me give you a personal illustration. My grandfather lived in Northern Ireland although he was Scottish. Even in his day they were fighting, and he didn't like it. So he emigrated to the United States. Now, what my grandfather did, I did. When he left Northern Ireland, I left Northern Ireland. And I thank God he left. I really appreciate what Grandpa did for me! What he did, I did because I was in him. The reason I was born in America is because of what he had done.

In this same way Adam's sin is imputed to us.

We have already seen that the righteousness of Christ is imputed to us by the death of Christ. Christ is the head of a new race, a new redeemed man, and the church is His body, a new creation. The hymn writer put it accurately: "The Church's one foundation is Jesus Christ her Lord. She is His new creation by water and the word." The church is a new creation, a new race. This is what Paul says, "And so it is written, The first man Adam was made a living soul; the last Adam was made a quickening spirit. . . . The first man is of the earth, earthy: the second man is the Lord from heaven" (1 Cor. 15:45, 47). Now, there will not be a third Adam, for Christ is the *last* Adam. There will be the third and fourth and myriads of *men* because Christ is the second man, but He's not the second Adam. He is the *last* Adam. He is the *head* of a new race. That is something that is preliminary.

As we go through this section, we will notice an expression that is very meaningful. It is "much more." What Paul is going to say is that we have "much more" in Christ than we *lost* in Adam. That expression occurred in verse 9, "Much more then, being now justified by his blood, we shall be saved from wrath through him." And in verse 10, "Much more, being reconciled, we shall be saved by his life." There is a great deal of "much more" in this section. In 1 Corinthians 15, verses 21–22, I read this, "For since by man came death, by man came also the resurrection of the dead. For as in Adam all die, even so in Christ shall all be made alive." Now, death came by Adam. And if you want proof that the first sin of Adam was a representative act, consider why a little infant will die when that little child has not committed a sinful act. Well, that little infant belongs to the race of Adam. In Adam all die. You see, God did not create man to die. God had something better in store for man and does today.

Now, with that thought in mind, let's move on to verse 13.

**(For until the law sin was in the world: but sin is not imputed when there is no law [Rom. 5:13].**

From Adam to Moses sin was in the world, but at that time sin was not a transgression; it was merely rebellion against God. I think this is the reason God did not exact the death penalty from Cain when he murdered his brother. I cannot think of a deed more dastardly than what he did, but at that time God had not yet said, "Thou shalt not kill"

(Exod. 20:13). Actually, God put a mark on Cain to protect him. A little later on you find that one of the sons of Cain, Lamech, tells why he killed a man. He says, "I have slain a man to my wounding, and a young man to my hurt. If Cain shall be avenged sevenfold, truly Lamech seventy and sevenfold" (Gen. 4:23–24). You see, Lamech had a reason. Also, that generation that was destroyed at the Flood was saturated with sin. They were incurable incorrigibles. "And GOD saw that the wickedness of man was great in the earth, and that every imagination of the thoughts of his heart was only evil continually" (Gen. 6:5). But not one of them broke the Ten Commandments—because there were no Ten Commandments then. But they were judged because they were sinners. And, friend, that answers the question about the heathen being lost who haven't heard the gospel. The answer is that all men belong to a lost race. It may be difficult for you and me to accept this fact, but you and I have been born into a lost race. We're not a lovely people. We are not the product of evolution—onward and upward forever with everything getting better. You and I belong to a lost race, and we need to be redeemed. Even the very thoughtlife of man is alienated from God.

Somebody may say, "Then I think God is obligated to save all of us." No, He is not. Suppose that you could go down to an old marshy lake covered with scum where there are hundreds of turtles, and you take a turtle out of there. And you teach this turtle to fly. Then this turtle goes back to the lake and says to the other turtles, "Wouldn't you like to learn to fly?" I think they'd laugh at the turtle. They'd say, "No! we like it down here. We don't want to learn to fly." And that is the condition of lost mankind today. People don't want to be saved. People are lost, alienated from God. Now, that's a great truth that does not soak into our minds easily, because we have that lost nature. We just love to think that we're wonderful people. But we are *not*, my friend.

**Nevertheless death reigned from Adam to Moses, even over them that had not sinned after the similitude of Adam's transgression, who is the figure of him that was to come [Rom. 5:14].**

Paul is personifying death. He speaks of the fact that death reigned like a king from Adam to Moses. Although he had not broken the Ten Commandments—because they hadn't yet been given—man was yet a sinner.

The word *death* is used in a threefold way in Scripture. There is what is known as physical death. That refers only to the body, and it means a separation of the spirit from the body. This death comes to man because of Adam's sin. Also, there is spiritual death, which is separation from and rebellion against God. And we inherit this nature from Adam, by the way. We are alienated from God, and we are dead in trespasses and sins (see Eph. 2:1). That is the picture that Scripture presents. Then there is eternal death. That is the third death that Scripture speaks of, and it is eternal separation from God. And, unless man is redeemed, eternal death inevitably follows (see Rev. 21:8).

Adam is here definitely declared to be a type of Christ—"who is the figure" or "he is the type of him who was to come." That is, Adam is a type of Christ.

## HEADSHIP OF CHRIST

**But not as the offence, so also is the free gift. For if through the offence of one many be dead, much more the grace of God, and the gift by grace, which is by one man, Jesus Christ, hath abounded unto many [Rom. 5:15].**

We have "much more" in Christ. Today we are looking forward to something more wonderful than the Garden of Eden. As the writer of Hebrews tells us, "These all died in faith, not having received the promises, but having seen them afar off, and were persuaded of them, and embraced them, and confessed that they were strangers and pilgrims on the earth" (Heb. 11:13).

**And not as it was by one that sinned, so is the gift: for the judgment was by one to condemnation, but the free gift is of many offences unto justification [Rom. 5:16].**

Now I recognize that this is a difficult section, and this is one of the most difficult passages. To simplify it, all this section means is this: one transgression plunged the race into sin; and one act of obedience and the death of Christ upon the Cross makes it possible for lost man to be saved.

> **For if by one man's offence death reigned by one; much more they which receive abundance of grace and of the gift of righteousness shall reign in life by one, Jesus Christ.) [Rom. 5:17].**

Paul has previously stated (v. 14) that death reigns as king. Death came to the throne by one man who committed only one offense—that is, the original sin, the one act, involved the race. Here Paul presents another kingdom which is superior to the kingdom of death. It is the kingdom of life. It is offered to the subjects of the kingdom of death through the superabundance of grace. Man has only to receive it. The King of the kingdom of life is Jesus Christ. The gift comes through Him.

> **Therefore as by the offence of one judgment came upon all men to condemnation; even so by the righteousness of one the free gift came upon all men unto justification of life [Rom. 5:18].**

This is the underlying principle of the imputation of sin and the imputation of righteousness. This is the doctrine of the federal headship of the race in Adam and Christ.

> **For as by one man's disobedience many were made sinners, so by the obedience of one shall many be made righteous [Rom. 5:19].**

Here Paul sums up his argument on federal headship: Adam's one act of disobedience made all sinners—not just possessors of a sin nature, but guilty of the act of sin. Christ's obedience—His death and resurrection—makes it possible for God to declare righteous the sinner who believes in Him.

> **Moreover the law entered, that the offence might abound. But where sin abounded, grace did much more abound [Rom. 5:20].**

When God gave the Law, He gave with it a sacrificial system. Then later on Christ came to fulfill that part of it also. In other words, God has given to the human race, a lost race, an opportunity to be delivered from the guilt of sins—not the nature of sin. You and I will have that old sin nature throughout our lives.

> **That as sin hath reigned unto death, even so might grace reign through righteousness unto eternal life by Jesus Christ our Lord [Rom. 5:21].**

"As sin hath reigned unto death"—you and I are living in a world where sin reigns. Do you want to know who is king of the earth today? Well, Scripture tells us that Satan is the prince. He is the one who goes up and down this earth seeking whom he may devour (see 1 Pet. 5:8). "Sin hath reigned unto death," and the cemeteries are still being filled because of that.

"Even so might grace reign through righteousness unto eternal life by Jesus Christ our Lord." He is calling out a people—out of a lost race—and He is "teaching turtles to fly" if they want to. However, the turtle nature doesn't want to fly. Man is alienated from God; he has a sin nature. Now God offers salvation to a lost race.

The claims of God's righteousness are fully met in the death of Christ. The Kingdom is fully and firmly established on the Cross of Christ. All other ground is sinking sand. The believing sinner now has eternal life by being united to the last Adam, the raised and glorified Savior. This makes possible the sanctification of the saved sinner, which is the theme of the next chapter.

# CHAPTER 6

***THEME:*** *Positional sanctification; practical sanctification*

We discovered in chapter 5 that sin has come through the headship of Adam and that sanctification comes through the headship of Christ. Because of the natural headship of Adam, sin was imputed to the human family. But there is another head of the human family, and that is Christ. He brings life and righteousness. He removes the guilt of sin from us. And on that basis, He can move into the lives of those who trust in Him and begin to make them righteous. That is, He can begin to make them *good.*

Now here in chapter 6 we begin with what I have labeled "positional sanctification."

Let me say a word about this matter of sanctification. There is a difference between justification and sanctification. These are two words from the Bible, my friend, that you ought to cozy up to and get acquainted with. There is a difference between merely being saved from sin and being made the type of folk we should be because we are separated unto God.

Identification with Christ for justification is also the grounds of our sanctification. We are in Christ. These are two different subjects, but they are not mutually exclusive. Justification is the foundation on which all the superstructure of sanctification rests.

Now let me put it like this: justification is an *act;* sanctification is a *work.* Justification took place the moment you trusted Christ—you were declared righteous; the guilt was removed. Then God began a work in you that will continue throughout your life. I believe in instantaneous salvation, but sanctification is a lifelong process. In other words, justification is the means; sanctification is the end. Justification is *for* us; sanctification is *in* us. Justification *declares* the sinner righteous; sactification *makes* the sinner righteous. Justification removes the *guilt* and *penalty* of sin; sanctification removes the *growth* and the *power* of sin.

God is both an exterior and interior decorator. He is an exterior decorator in that He enables us to stand before Him because He has paid the penalty and removed the guilt of sin from us. But He is also an interior decorator. He moves into our hearts and lives by the power of the Holy Spirit to make us the kind of Christians we should be. God does not leave us in sin when He saves us.

This does not imply that sanctification is a duty that is derived from justification. It is a fact that proceeds from it, or rather, both justification and sanctification flow from being in Christ, crucified and risen. The sinner appropriates Christ by faith for both his salvation and his sanctification. We're told in 1 Corinthians 1:30, "But of him are ye in Christ Jesus, who of God is made unto us wisdom, and righteousness, and sanctification, and redemption."

Up to chapter 6, Paul does not discuss the *holy life* of the saint. From chapter 6 on, Paul does not discuss the salvation of the sinner. He wasn't talking about the saint and the life he is to live when he was discussing salvation. Now he *is* discussing that. Therefore, the subject of this chapter is the ability of God to make sinners, whom He has declared righteous, actually righteous. He shows that the justified sinner cannot continue in sin because he died and rose again in Christ. To continue in sin leads to slavery to sin and is the additional reason for not continuing in sin. The believer has a new nature now, and he is to obey God. This section delivers us from the prevalent idea today that a believer can do as he pleases. Union with Christ in His death and resurrection means that He is now our Lord and our Master. He gives us freedom, but that freedom is not license, as we are going to see.

## POSITIONAL SANCTIFICATION

**What shall we say then? Shall we continue in sin, that grace may abound? [Rom. 6:1].**

Paul is being argumentative. He wasn't, you remember, when he was discussing sin. Rather, he was stating facts. He wasn't trying to prove anything. He just looked at life in the raw, right down where the rubber meets the road, and said that we are all sinners. However, now he uses this idiomatic question which opens this chapter, and he is argumentative. In the Greek the question is asked in such a way that there is only one answer. He precedes the question with "What shall we say then?" After you see God's wonderful salvation, what can you say to it? Our only fitting response is hallelujah! What else can you say to God's wonderful salvation? Now Paul's argumentative question is this: "Shall we continue in sin, that grace may abound?"

And this, my friend, is God's answer to the question of whether, after we are saved, we can continue to live in sin. The answer is, "God forbid" or "perish the thought!" or "may it never be!"

**God forbid. How shall we, that are dead to sin, live any longer therein? [Rom. 6:2].**

The very fact that Paul is asking this question makes it obvious that he understood justification to mean a *declaration* of righteousness; that it did not mean to *make* a person good, but to *declare* a person good. Justification means that the guilt or the penalty of sin is removed, not the power of sin in this life.

Now he is going to talk about removing the *power* of sin. If God has declared you to be righteous and has removed the guilt of your sin, then, my friend, you cannot continue in sin. The answer is, "God forbid!"

"How shall we, that are dead to sin"—this is something that is misunderstood. We are never *dead* to sin as long as we are in this life. The literal translation is, "How shall we who have *died* to sin." Note this distinction. That means we died in the person of our substitute, Jesus Christ. We died to sin in Christ. But we are never *dead* to sin. Any honest person knows he never reaches the place where he is dead to sin. He does reach the place where he wants to live for God, but he recognizes he still has that old sin nature.

It is verses like that that have led a group of sincere folk, whom I call super–duper saints—I hope I'm not being unfair to them—to feel they have reached an exalted plane where they do not commit sin. One such group is a branch of those who teach the "victorious life."

They feel they have reached the pinnacle of perfection. There are different brands of these, I know, but one group was especially obnoxious several years ago in Southern California. One young man approached me following a morning worship service, and he asked, "Are you living the victorious life?" I think I shocked him when I said, "No, I'm not!" Then I asked him, "Are you?" Well, he beat around the bush and didn't want to give me a direct answer. He said he tried to. And I said, "Wait a minute, that's not the question. You asked me if I am living it, and I said no. Now you answer me yes or no." And to this good day he hasn't answered me. Like most of them, he was a very anemic–looking fellow; I suspected he was a fugitive from a blood bank. He continued arguing his case. "Well, doesn't the Scripture say, 'I am crucified with Christ?' and doesn't it say that we are dead to sin?" I said, "No, that is not what the Scriptures say. We *died* to sin in Christ—that's our position—but we are never dead to sin in this life. You have a sinful nature; I have a sinful nature; and we'll have it as long as we are in this life." He persisted, "Then what does it mean when it says we are crucified with Christ?" So I told him, "When Christ died over nineteen hundred years ago, that is when we died. We died in Him, and we were raised in Him, and we are joined now to a living Christ. This is the great truth that is there. I don't know about you, but I'm not able to crucify myself. The very interesting thing is that you can kill yourself in a variety of ways—by poison, with a gun, by jumping off a building—but you cannot crucify yourself. Maybe you can drive the nails into one hand on a cross, but how are you going to fasten the other hand to the cross? You cannot do it. How are you going to crucify yourself? You cannot do it. My young friend, you were crucified over nineteen hundred years ago when Christ died."

**Know ye not, that so many of us as were baptized into Jesus Christ were baptized into this death? [Rom. 6:3].**

This again is a verse that has been misunderstood. If you find water in this verse, you have missed the meaning.

Many years ago the late Dr. William L. Pettingill was conducting a conference in the church I was pastoring, and as I was driving him back to the hotel after a service, I said, "Dr. Pettingill, did I understand you to say there is no water in the sixth chapter of Romans?" (I should add that he was the strongest "immersionist" I have ever met in my life.) He laughed and said, "No, that's not exactly what I said. I said that if all you see in Romans 6 is water, you have missed the point." I said, "Well, if you go that far, that is wonderful for me because it confirms the great truth that is here."

What did Paul mean by the word *baptize* in this third verse? I do not think he refers to water baptism primarily. Don't misunderstand me; I believe in water baptism, and I believe that immersion best sets forth what is taught here. But actually he is talking about identification with Christ. You see, the translators did not translate the Greek word *baptiz*, they merely transliterated it. That is they just spelled the Greek word out in English, because *baptiz* has so many meanings. In my Greek lexicon there are about twenty meanings for this word. Actually *baptiz* could refer to dyeing your hair. In fact, there was a group in Asia Minor who dyed their hair purple; and they belonged to a *bapti* group. But here in Romans 6:3 Paul is speaking about identification with Jesus Christ. We were baptized or identified into His death. In 1 Corinthians 12:13 Paul says, "For by one Spirit are we all baptized into one body . . . ." We are identified in the death of Christ, as Paul will explain in the next verse.

Now Paul is going to say that there are three things essential to our santification. Two of them are positional; one of them is very practical. For the two that are positional, we are to *know* something. Every gadget that you buy has instructions with it. When I buy a toy for one of my grandsons, I take it out of the box, and I try to follow instructions for assembling it—and sometimes it is very difficult for me to do. Well, living the Christian life is such an important thing that it comes with instructions. There are certainly things we are to know. We are to know that when Christ died over nineteen hundred years ago, we were identified with Him. Let me make it personal. Nineteen hundred years ago, they led me outside of an oriental city by the name of Jerusalem. By the way, I stood at that spot not too long ago. I looked up to Gordon's Calvary, the Place of the Skull, Golgotha. I tried to visualize the One who died there. When He died there over nineteen hundred years ago, He took Vernon McGee there. I was the one who was guilty. He was not guilty. Don't argue with me about whether the Jews crucified Christ—He died on the Roman cross—but let's not argue that. My sin put Him up there, and your sin put Him up there, my friend. We were identified with Jesus Christ. That is something that we should know, and it is very important for us to know. We're identified with him.

Now Paul will amplify this:

> **Therefore we are buried with him by baptism into death: that like as Christ was raised up from the dead by the glory of the Father, even so we also should walk in newness of life [Rom. 6:4].**

"We are buried with him by baptism into death"—just as we are identified with Christ in His death, likewise are we identified with Christ in His resurrection. We are joined today to a living Christ. In other words, our sins have already been judged; we are already raised; and we are yonder seated with Christ in the heavenlies. My friend, there are only two places for your sins: either they were on Christ when he died for you over nineteen hundred years ago—because you have trusted Him as your Savior—or they are on you today, and judgment is ahead for you. There is no third place for them.

"We are buried with him by baptism [identification] into [His] death." Frankly, although I was reared a Presbyterian, I think that immersion is a more accurate type of this identification. I think the Spirit's baptism is the real baptism. Water is the ritual baptism, but I do think that immersion sets forth the great spiritual truth that is here. This is the reason a child of God should be baptized in water in our day. It is a testimony that he is joined to the living Christ. That is all important.

What did Peter mean when he said in 1 Peter 3:21, ". . . baptism doth also now save us . . ."? How does it save us? Well, in the preceding verse he talks about eight souls who were saved in the ark. They went through the waters of judgment inside the ark. The folk in the water were those who were outside the ark, and they were drowned. The eight people in the ark didn't get wet at all—yet Peter says they were saved by baptism. Obviously the word *baptism* has nothing to do with water in this instance; rather it means identification. They were identified with the ark. They had believed God, and they had gotten into the ark. God saw that little boat floating on the surface of the water. Now today God sees Christ; He doesn't see Vernon McGee because I am in Christ. He is my ark today. Christ went down into the waters of death, and we are in Christ. And we are raised with Him. We are joined to Him. This is important. Don't miss it. If you do, you will miss one of the greatest truths of the Christian life.

**For if we have been planted together in the likeness of his death, we shall be also in the likeness of his resurrection [Rom. 6:5].**

In other words, if we are united by being grafted together in the likeness of His death, we shall be also united by growth—grafted, vitally connected—in the likeness of His resurrection. We actually share the life of Christ somewhat as a limb grafted into a tree shares the life of the tree. The life of Christ is our life now.

**Knowing this, that our old man is crucified with him, that the body of sin might be destroyed, that henceforth we should not serve sin [Rom. 6:6].**

"Knowing this"—these are things we know.

When Paul says your "old man" is crucified with Him, he doesn't mean your father; he means your old nature is crucified with Him. "That the body of sin might be destroyed"—the word *destroyed* is *katargeo*, meaning "to make of none effect, to be paralyzed or canceled or nullified"—"that henceforth we should not serve sin." Paul is not saying that the old nature is eradicated. He is saying that since the old man was crucified, the body of sin has been put out of business, so that from now on we should not be in bondage to sin.

**For he that is dead is freed from sin [Rom. 6:7].**

For he who died is declared righteous from sin. He is acquitted. That is his position.

> **Now if we be dead with Christ, we believe that we shall also live with him [Rom. 6:8].**

If we died with Christ, we believe that we shall also be living with Him both here and hereafter. We share His resurrection life today, and we will be raised from the dead someday.

> **Knowing that Christ being raised from the dead dieth no more; death hath no more dominion over him [Rom. 6:9].**

"Knowing"—this is something else we are to know.

"He ever liveth" is the visitor's chorus. The glorified Christ says, "I am he that liveth, and was dead; and, behold, I am alive for evermore, Amen; and have the keys of hell and of death" (Rev. 1:18). The Resurrection opens up eternity to Christ, and it will open up eternity to those who will trust Him.

> **For in that he died, he died unto sin once: but in that he liveth, he liveth unto God [Rom. 6:10].**

He died one time, but He is alive today. And He ever lives to make intercession for those who are His. Because of this, He can save you right through to the utmost.

Now we come to the second thing that we as believers are to reckon on.

> **Likewise reckon ye also yourselves to be dead indeed unto sin, but alive unto God through Jesus Christ our Lord [Rom. 6:11].**

"Reckon" doesn't mean I "reckon" or "suppose," as some of us Texans use it. Rather, we are to *count* on the fact that we are dead unto sin and alive unto God. We are to reckon (count on it) that our old nature lay in Joseph's tomb over nineteen hundred years ago, but when Christ came back from the dead, we came back from the dead in Him. This is something to count on.

> **Let not sin therefore reign in your mortal body, that ye should obey it in the lusts thereof [Rom. 6:12].**

That is, don't let sin keep on reigning in your body, that you should obey the desires of the body.

## PRACTICAL SANCTIFICATION

We have seen that sanctification is positional. That means we are to know something. We are to know God's method of making a sinner the kind of person He wants him to be. While justification merely declared him righteous, removed the *guilt* of sin, it did not change him in his life. It gave him a new nature. Now he is to know that he was buried with Christ and raised with Him. God wants him to live in the power of the Holy Spirit. The believer is joined to the living Christ. He is to reckon on that fact; he is to count on it. He is to consider it as true. You too, God saved us by faith, and we are to live by faith. Many of us, and that includes this poor preacher, have trusted Him for salvation, but are we trusting Him in our daily living? We are to live by faith.

Now we come to that which is very practical indeed. You are to yield yourself or present yourself to God.

> **Neither yield ye your members as instruments of unrighteousness unto sin: but yield yourselves unto God, as those that are alive from the dead, and your members as instruments of righteousness unto God [Rom. 6:13].**

*Yield* is the same word as *present* in Romans 12:1; "I beseech you therefore, brethren, by the mercies of God, that ye present your bodies a living sacrifice, holy, acceptable unto God . . . ." This is a presentation of yourself for service. *Yield* is the same word, and it means "to present yourself." The idea of the surrendered life or the yielded life sounds colorless to so many people. We talk about surrendering and at the same time living the victorious life, and they seem to be a contradiction of terms. I like the word *present* much better—"Neither present ye your members as instruments of unrighteousness unto sin." The reason most of us get into trouble is because we yield ourselves to the old nature. By an act of the will we can yield ourselves to do God's will through the new nature.

A little girl fell out of bed one night and began to cry. Her mother rushed into her bedroom, picked her up, put her back in bed, and asked her, "Honey, why did you fall out of bed?" And she said, "I think I stayed too close to the place where I got in." And that's the reason a great many of us fall, my friend. It is because we are actually yielding ourselves to the old nature. We're following the dictates of the old nature; that is what gets us into trouble.

Although we will not get rid of that old nature in this life, we are told now, "Yield yourselves unto God." Just as you yield yourself to do sin, you are to yield yourself unto God "as those that are alive from the dead." You're now alive in Christ. You have a new nature. You've been born again.

"And your members as instruments of righteousness unto God" deals with that which is specific and particular. What is your real problem, friend? I know what mine is. What about yours? Whatever that specific thing is, yield it to God. A bad temper? Well, take that to Him and talk to Him about it. What about a gossipy tongue? A dear lady who attended a "tongues meeting" was asked if she wanted to speak in tongues. She exclaimed, "Oh, my no. I'd like to lose about forty feet off the one I have now!" If your tongue is your problem, yield it to God. And by the way, in this day in which we are living, what about immorality? Sex is the big subject of the hour. My, everybody's getting in on the act today. Is that your sin? Well, you're to yield yourself to God—your members "as instruments of righteousness unto God." And don't tell me you can't do it. You can do it through the power of the Holy Spirit.

**For sin shall not have dominion over you: for ye are not
under the law, but under grace [Rom. 6:14].**

The Law was given to control the old nature. As a believer, you are not
to live by the old nature. You have a new nature, and you are to yield
yourself or present yourself to God. What a glorious, wonderful privilege it is to present ourselves to Him!

**What then? shall we sin, because we are not under the
law, but under grace? God forbid [Rom 6:15].**

Let me give my translation of this verse, which may be helpful: What
then? Shall we sin, because we are not under law, but under grace?
(Should we commit an act of sin? For you are no more under law, but
under grace.) Away with the thought (perish the thought). The form of
the question is put differently here than it was back in verse 1. Paul
has demonstrated in the past fourteen verses that God's method of
sanctification is on the same basis as justification; it is by faith, faith
that God can do it. You and I *cannot* do it. When we learn that we
cannot live the Christian life, we have learned a great lesson. Then we
are prepared to let Him live it through us.

Paul's question here is whether there should be an assist given to
grace to accomplish its high and holy end. In other words, the natural
man thinks there ought to be some laws, rules, or regulations given.
In the course of the church's history we have had all kinds of groups
that have come up with rules for living the Christian life. There were
the Puritans, a wonderful group of folk, and we owe a great deal to
them, but they had a strict observance of the Sabbath Day (they called
Sunday the Sabbath, which, of course, it is not). A strict observance of
Sunday was an obsession with them. We have a carry-over of that
today. There are a great number of groups who put down certain rules
for a believer. Some of our fundamental people have made, not ten commandments, but about twenty new commandments. If the believer does
certain things and refrains from doing certain other things, he is living
the Christian life. This is the reason, friend, that I oppose the idea that

you can become a wonderful Christian by taking some of these short courses being offered today. That's not the way you are to do it. We have a girl in our office who took a course, and, oh, she was enthusiastic. But you ought to see her today. She is really in a depression. Why? Because she tried to do it by rules and did not let Christ do it.

The Christian life is not following certain rules; you can follow rules and regulations and still not be living the Christian life. Somebody asks, "Then what is the Christian life?" The Christian life is to be *obedient* unto *Christ*. It means communication with Christ. My friend, do you love Him? That's the important thing. He says, "If ye *love* me, keep my commandments" (John 14:15, italics mine). Identification with Christ is positional sanctification, as we have seen. That is basic. But obedience to Christ is the *experience* of sanctification, and that is practical sanctification. It is just as simple as that, my friend. It is not *how* you walk, but *where* you walk—are you walking in the light, walking in fellowship with Christ? Sin will break the fellowship, of course, and then we are to confess our sin. The Lord Jesus said to Peter yonder in the Upper Room, "If I wash you not, you have no part with me" (see John 13:8). We don't have fellowship with Him unless we confess our sins to Him as we go along. Our part is confession; His part is cleansing (see 1 John 1:9). The important thing for you and me is to have fellowship with the Lord Jesus Christ and to obey Him. Then we will be living the Christian life.

Vincent once said to Godet, "There is a subtle poison which insinuates itself into the heart even of the best Christian; it is the temptation to say: Let us sin, not that grace may abound, but because it abounds." You see, there are many Christians today who say, "I am saved, and I can do as I please." My friend, if you have been saved by grace, you cannot do as you please, as we shall see in the eighth chapter of Romans.

In his letter to the Galatian believers, Paul makes it clear that there are three ways in which you can live: (1) You can live by law; (2) you can live by license; (3) you can live by liberty. To live by law, everyone puts down some principle. I read of a movie star who said that his whole life was given to sex—that's his law; he lives by that. Regardless of who you are, if you are living by law, you are living by the old nature. Then, the other extreme which Paul is guarding against here, is license. If you are a child of God, you can't do as you please; you have to do as Christ pleases. You must be obedient to the Lord Jesus Christ, present yourself to Him. This is practical, a great deal more practical than you may realize.

**Know ye not, that to whom ye yield yourselves servants to obey, his servants ye are to whom ye obey; whether of sin unto death, or of obedience unto righteousness? [Rom. 6:16].**

"Know ye not"—when Paul says this, we can be sure that we believers *don't* know, and we need to know.

"To whom ye yield yourselves servants to obey, his servants ye are." Every person who is living is a bond servant to someone or something. I heard a contemporary commentator observe that every person obeys some person or some thing. That is true. You could even be obeying Satan himself. Because of our very natures, we are servants or slaves to something or to somebody.

Now Paul is saying here that the one who is our master is the one whom we obey. If you obey sin, then that is your master. Don't say Christ is your master if you are living in sin; He is *not* your master. He brings you into the place of liberty. "If the Son therefore shall make you free, ye shall be free indeed" (John 8:36)—free to do what? You will be free to live for Him, free to obey Him. And the Lord Jesus said again, ". . . Verily, verily, I say unto you. Whosoever committeth sin is the servant of sin" (John 8:34). Now let me use a very homely illustration. There is a very swanky club across the street from the church I served in downtown Los Angeles. It is made up of rich men, and I'm told that it costs several thousand dollars to join this club. If you belong to it, you probably own a Cadillac and have a chauffeur. Well, one day as I looked out the window, I saw a group of chauffeurs standing around talking, and there were several Cadillacs parked there. It was after lunch. Finally, I saw a very distinguished-looking gentleman come out of the club; he made a motion and said something. I couldn't hear what he said, but I saw one of the chauffeurs leave the group of about fifteen men. He went over, opened the door of the car, the distinguished-looking man got in, then he went around, got in the driver's seat and drove off. Now, I came to a very profound conclusion: that chauffeur was the servant or the employee of the man who called him. I don't think those other fourteen chauffeurs were employed by the man in the car because they didn't obey him. Only the man who obeyed him was working for him. He obeyed him because that man was his master. This is what Paul is saying. Regardless of who you are, whomever you obey, whatever you obey, that is your master. You are obeying something or someone.

Now that brings us to a personal question. Is Christ really our master today? Just because you don't murder, you don't lie, you don't do other things the Mosaic Law prohibits, doesn't mean you are living the Christian life. It may mean you are living a good life, but that is all. The Christian life is one where we obey Christ.

> **But God be thanked, that ye were the servants of sin, but ye have obeyed from the heart that form of doctrine which was delivered you [Rom. 6:17].**

In other words, when you were in the world, when you were lost, you obeyed sin. It was natural for you to do that. A man may live such an exemplary life that the chamber of commerce presents him with a medal and a loving cup and makes him the citizen of the year. I overheard such a man talking one time after he had been presented with the cup as the outstanding citizen of a certain community. The language of this man was the foulest language I had ever heard. He may be the outstanding citizen of that community, but it's quite obvious whom he's obeying. He is obeying the Devil! The fact that you obey Christ is the thing that is important.

Now, another thing that we need to understand is that, when you have been saved, you have a new nature that *can* obey Christ. Paul went through the experience, as we shall see in the next chapter, of being a new Christian and discovering that there was no good in his old nature. Paul says "I know that in me (that is, in my flesh,) dwelleth no good thing" (Rom. 7:18). Although many of us have not discovered this, there is no good in us; the old nature has no good in it. You can do a lot to improve it, but you sure can't make it good.

The second startling fact is this: there is no power in the new nature. That's where most of us make our mistake. We think that because we are now Christians, we can walk on top of the world. We can't. We are just as weak as we've ever been before. This is the reason that we have to walk by faith and in the power of the Holy Spirit. Only the Spirit of God can produce the Christian life, as we shall see.

**Being then made free from sin, ye became the servants of righteousness [Rom. 6:18].**

We have been liberated. In other words, He has made it possible for us to live the Christian life. It does not mean that sin has been eradicated or removed. It does mean that now we can live for God.

**I speak after the manner of men because of the infirmity of your flesh: for as ye have yielded your members servants to uncleanness and to iniquity unto iniquity; even so now yield your members servants to righteousness unto holiness [Rom. 6:19].**

Let me give you my translation of this verse: I speak in human terms on account of the difficulties of apprehension or the weakness of your human nature; for as you presented or yielded your members slaves for the practice of impurity and to lawlessness; even so now present your members slaves to righteousness.

Paul explains here, I think, why he uses the term *servants*. He half-way apologizes in the last verse for using it. Slavery was common in the Roman Empire. Out of the 120 million people in the Roman Empire, one-half were slaves. Many Christians were slaves. And the little Epistle to Philemon reveals that freedom was a prized possession and difficult to obtain. Now Paul uses this familiar metaphor which he describes as "human terms." He doesn't mean he is not speaking by inspiration, but he is speaking in a manner which we will understand. And we will understand by these human terms that we are actually slaves.

Now, the religious rulers were insulted when the Lord suggested that they were slaves of sin. Remember the Lord Jesus said to those Jews that believed on Him, ". . . If ye continue in my word, then are ye my disciples indeed; and ye shall know the truth, and the truth shall make you free. They answered him, We be Abraham's seed, and were never in bondage to any man: how sayest thou, Ye shall be made free? Jesus answered them, Verily, verily, I say unto you, Whosoever committeth sin is the servant of sin" (John 8:31–34). Oh, how many men and women today are slaves of sin! Observe the tragedy of our young people who have rebelled against the rules and regulations of the establishment and who have been destroyed by the thousands by drugs and alcohol! You may be delivered from one group with its rules and regulations, but if you don't turn to Christ, you may be getting out of the frying pan and into the fire. What is happening in our culture today is one of the saddest things of our contemporary age. The Lord Jesus says that when you commit sin, you are the servant of sin.

**For when ye were the servants of sin, ye were free from righteousness [Rom. 6:20].**

That is, you don't think of serving Christ then; you weren't interested in that. You were free from Him.

**What fruit had ye then in those things whereof ye are now ashamed? for the end of those things is death [Rom. 6:21].**

You were not only free from Christ, you were fruitless. You did as you pleased. The only fruit was shame. Actually, it was not real freedom, it was license. Do you want to go back to the old life?

I receive scores of letters from young people who were formerly known as "hippies" and have turned to Christ. They are ashamed of that old life. When you drop into sin, does it break your heart? The difference between a child of God and a child of the Devil is that a child of the Devil just loves doing what the Devil wants done. But to the child of God it is a heartbreak.

**But now being made free from sin, and become servants to God, ye have your fruit unto holiness, and the end everlasting life [Rom. 6:22].**

He sets before believers now the golden and glad prospect that is theirs as slaves of God. They are freed from sin which leads to death, and they can have fruit which will abide into eternity. Life eternal is in contrast to death. An illustration of this is seen in the lives of pioneer missionaries. I think of the group of young people, some of them still in their teens, who went out to the Hawaiian Islands in 1819. They gave their lives gladly, joyfully, to the service of Christ. (They have been maligned in recent years. Oh, how the godless tourist loves to hear them ridiculed!) But they laid the foundation for the greatest revival that has taken place since Pentecost—more people were won to Christ per capita. I never grow weary of hearing their story. They had fruit, my friend. How wonderful it was!

**For the wages of sin is death; but the gift of God is eternal life through Jesus Christ our Lord [Rom. 6:23].**

The Devil is the paymaster, and he will see to it that you get paid. If you work for him, the wages of sin is death. But the gift of God is eternal life. And you will receive that gift by faith.

You are saved by faith. You are to live by faith. You are to walk moment by moment by faith. You cannot live for God by yourself any more than you can save yourself. It requires constant dependence upon Him, looking to the Lord Jesus Christ by the power of the Spirit.

# CHAPTER 7

*THEME:* Shackles of a saved soul; struggle of a saved soul

The theme of sanctification began in the latter part of chapter 5 where it was "potential sanctification." Then in chapter 6 we saw "positional sanctification"; that is, identification with Christ in His death and resurrection. We are to reckon on that, present ourselves to Him, and trust him to live the Christian life through us.

Now in the chapter before us there are two subjects: the shackles of a saved soul and the struggle of a saved soul. The Law cannot produce sanctification in the life of the believer; it merely shackles it. Neither can the believer produce sanctification in his life by depending on the desire of the new nature. Just to say you want to live for Christ won't get you anywhere. You need to present yourself to Him, recognizing that you are joined to the living Christ.

The importance of this chapter cannot be overemphasized. Let me give you a quotation from Dr. Griffith Thomas: "Dr. Alexander Whyte once said that whenever a new book on Romans comes out and is sent to him by its publisher for consideration, he at once turns to the comments on chapter VII, and according to the view taken of that important section he decides on the value of the entire work." Then Dr. Frederic Godet makes this bold statement: "But it is a hundred to one when a reader does not find the Apostle Paul logical, that he is not understanding his thought." Paul is certainly logical all through this chapter.

When I was a young man, a very wonderful itinerant Bible teacher, who was a great blessing to multitudes of folk, was a great help to me. He was never a pastor, and he taught that we are to detour around the seventh chapter of Romans; we are not to live there. We are to get into the eighth chapter of Romans. For several years I taught that philosophy also. But I have now been a pastor for a long time, and I have come to the conclusion that we are not to miss the seventh chapter of Romans. I am sure that many a pastor wishes his church members would get into the seventh of Romans, because the man who gets into the seventh of Romans will get into the eighth of Romans. I am of the opinion that the way into the eighth chapter is through the seventh chapter—at least that is the route most of us take. Well, you are not to detour around it, because if you do, you are not on the direct route. It reminds me of a jingle:

> To dwell above
> With the saints in love—
> Oh, that will be glory!
> But to stay below
> With the saints I know—
> That's another story!

In this "struggle of a saved soul" a believer reaches out and grabs a straw. Sometimes that straw is the Mosaic Law. And he finds that he has gotten hold, not of a straw, nor even of a life preserver, but actually of a sack of cement, and it is pulling him under. He can't live that way. As a result, multitudes of the saints accept defeat as normal Christian living. There are many saints who are satisfied to continue on the low level of a sad, shoddy, sloppy life. God doesn't want us to come that route.

The "powerless sanctification" of this chapter shows us the way we are not to live. Many years ago a cartoon appeared in a daily paper—when it was popular to make things and repair things yourself—showing a mild-mannered man in a "Do-It-Yourself Shop." His hands were bandaged, and one arm was in a sling. He was asking the clerk behind the counter, "Do you have any undo-it-yourself kits?" Today we as believers need to know that we cannot live the Christian life; we need to learn that we cannot do it ourselves. In fact, we need an undo-it-yourself kit; that is, we need to turn our lives over to the Spirit of God, yield to Him, and let Him do for us what we cannot do ourselves.

The Mosaic Law is where many Christians go to try to find Christian living. Now Paul is going to show that the Mosaic Law has no claim on the believer. Actually, the Law condemned man to die; it was a ministration of condemnation (see 2 Cor. 3:9). You don't contact the judge who sentenced you to die and ask him how you are going to live!

## SHACKLES OF A SAVED SOUL

**Know ye not, brethren, (for I speak to them that know the law,) how that the law hath dominion over a man as long as he liveth? [Rom. 7:1].**

"Know ye not" is an expression that occurs again and again in the writings of Paul. Putting it into the positive, it is, "Are you so ignorant?" When Paul says, "Know ye not," you may be sure that the brethren did not know.

"I speak to them that know the law." The Mosaic Law had had over a millennium's trial with God's chosen people in a land that was favorable and adaptable to the keeping of the Law—the Law was not only given to a people but to a land. Yet Israel did not keep the Law. Remember that Stephen in his defense said that they had ". . . received the law by the disposition of angels, and have not kept it" (Acts 7:53). Peter calls it a yoke "which neither our fathers nor we were able to bear" (Acts 15:10).

Now Paul will give an illustration that I think is a great one. Unfortunately folk try to draw from it rules for marriage and divorce. But Paul is not talking about marriage and divorce here. Rather, he is illustrating by a well-established and stated law that a wife is bound to a living husband and that death frees her from the status of wife.

**For the woman which hath an husband is bound by the law to her husband so long as he liveth; but if the husband be dead, she is loosed from the law of her husband [Rom. 7:2].**

A wife is bound to her husband as long as he lives, but when the husband dies, she is completely discharged from the law of her husband. In other words, if he is dead, she is no longer married to him.

**So then if, while her husband liveth, she be married to another man, she shall be called an adulteress: but if her husband be dead, she is free from that law; so that she is no adulteress, though she be married to another man [Rom. 7:3].**

Some folk insist that divorce and remarriage is not permitted under any circumstances according to this verse. We need to thoroughly understand the background. What would happen under the Mosaic Law if a man or woman were unfaithful in marriage? Suppose a woman is married to a man who is a philanderer, and he is unfaithful to her. What happens? He is stoned to death. When the old boy is lying under a pile of stones, she is free to marry another, of course. In our day we cannot apply the Mosaic Law—we can't stone to death the unfaithful. And Paul is not giving us instructions on divorce and remarriage here; he will do that elsewhere. The point Paul is making here is that when a woman's husband dies, she is no longer a wife, she is a single woman again. This is, I think, a universal principle among civilized people. There are heathen people who put the wife to death when the husband dies, but civilized folk have never followed that practice.

Paul goes on to amplify the law of husband and wife. He brings into sharp focus her status in the case that her husband is alive and again in the case that the husband is dead.

**Wherefore, my brethren, ye also are become dead to the law by the body of Christ; that ye should be married to another, even to him who is raised from the dead, that we should bring forth fruit unto God [Rom. 7:4].**

In other words: Accordingly, my brethren, you (old Adamic nature) also were done to death as to the Law; the Law was killed to you by means of the body of Christ; that you should be married to another, even to Him who rose from the dead, that we might bear fruit unto God.

The wife represents the believer in Christ. The second husband represents Christ. We are joined to Him. But who is the first husband?

Let's see what some have said. Dr. William Sanday interprets him as the old state before conversion: "The (first) Husband—the old state before conversion to Christianity." Dr. Stifler concludes that the first husband is Christ crucified. Dr. William R. Newell held that the first husband set forth Adam and our position in him.

Personally, I consider the latter the best interpretation, because all the way through this section, beginning at chapter 5 where there were two headships—Adam and Christ—we have seen the first Adam and the last Adam, the first man and the second man. We are joined to Adam through the old Adamic nature. The Law was given to control the old Adamic nature, but it failed through the infirmity of the flesh. The Law actually became a millstone around the neck of the Israelite. It never lifted him up, but it kept him in slavery for fifteen hundred years. Its demands had to be met, but man could not meet them. It was indeed a ministration of condemnation. If the Gentile had to adopt the Law when he became a believer, there was no hope for him either. Paul says that Christ died in His body, we are identified with Christ in His death, and now we are dead to the Law and the Law is dead to us. That first husband is Adam, and we are no longer joined to him. Now we are joined to the living Christ. We died with Him and we have been raised with Him. He is the second husband, the living Christ, who enables us to bear fruit. We know Christ no longer after the flesh; it is the *resurrected* Christ we are joined to. The Law is not given to the new man in Christ—old things have passed away and all things have become new (see 2 Cor. 5:17). The believer is not under law but under grace—this is the *ipso facto* statement of Scripture. Believer, *believe it!* It is so, for God says it!

Now let me illustrate this with a very ridiculous illustration that I heard when I was a student in seminary down in Georgia. Back in the antebellum days, before the Civil War, there was a plantation owner, a very fine, handsome man married to a beautiful woman, and they lived happily in a lovely home. Then he became sick and died suddenly. It was a great heartbreak to her, for she loved him dearly, and she did a strange and morbid thing. She had his body embalmed, placed in a sitting position in a chair in an air-tight glass case, and situated in the great hallway of her lovely southern home. The minute you opened the door, you were looking at him. Well, her friends realized that this wouldn't do, so they urged her to go away and travel for awhile. So she went north, then traveled abroad for almost two years. During that time she met another man, fell in love with him and married him. On their honeymoon they came to her plantation home. The new bridegroom did as a new bridegroom is supposed to do, he picked her up and carried her over the threshold. When he put her down, he was staring into the face of a man in a glass case. He said to his bride, "Who is *that?*" Well, she had forgotten about him. She told him that he was her first husband. They both decided it was time to bury him, which was the proper thing to do. She was married to a new man; the old man was dead. Now I confess that that is a ridiculous story; I sometimes wonder if it really ever happened. Whether or not the story is true, it *is* true that there are many believers today who have dug up the Law—in fact, they have never buried the Law. They have the Law sitting in a glass case, and they are trying to live by the Law in the strength of the old Adamic nature! How ridiculous! The believer is joined to the living Christ today, and the Christian's life is to please Him. Oh, how important that is. I can't overemphasize it.

**For when we were in the flesh, the motions of sins, which were by the law, did work in our members to bring forth fruit unto death [Rom. 7:5].**

Face this squarely, my friend. Are you able in your own strength to keep the Law? The Law was a straitjacket put on the flesh to control it. The flesh rebelled and chafed under the irksome restraint of the Law. The flesh had no capacity or desire to follow the injunctions of the Law. The flesh broke out of the restraint imposed by law and therefore brought down the irrevocable penalty for breaking the Law, which is death.

**But now we are delivered from the law, that being dead wherein we were held; that we should serve in newness of spirit, and not in the oldness of the letter [Rom. 7:6].**

"But now we are delivered from the law" means *discharged* or *annulled* from the Law. Notice the paradoxes in this section. In verse 4 it was having died, they bear fruit; here in verse 6 they have been discharged, yet they serve. Today we are to serve Him, not on the basis or the motive, "I ought to do it," but now, "I delight to do it because I want to please Christ." The believer is set free, but now in love he gives himself to the Savior as he never could do under the Law. Note this little bit of verse I used to carry in my Bible when I was a student in college and seminary:

> I do not work my soul to save;
>     That work my Lord hath done.
> But I will work like any slave
>     For love of God's dear Son.

We serve Christ because we love Him. Our Lord asked Simon Peter the direct question, ". . . Lovest thou me? . . ." (John 21:17). That is the question that faces you and me. God's question to the lost world is: "What will you do with My Son who died for you?" However, His question to the believer is: "Lovest thou me?"

The Christian life is Christ living His life through us today. We can't do it ourselves, nor can we do it by the law. There is nothing wrong with the Law—let's understand that—the problem is with us.

**What shall we say then? Is the law sin? God forbid. Nay, I had not known sin, but by the law: for I had not known lust, except the law had said, Thou shalt not covet.**

**But sin, taking occasion by the commandment, wrought in me all manner of concupiscence. For without the law sin was dead [Rom. 7:7–8].**

Let me try to bring out the meaning a little more clearly: What shall we say then? Is the Law sin? Away with the thought! On the contrary, I should not have been conscious of sin, except through law; for I had not known illicit desire (coveting). But sin, getting a start through the commandment, produced in me all manner of illicit desire. For apart from the Law sin is dead.

Paul, you recall, began his argument way back in the sixth chapter of Romans with this expression, "What shall we say then? Shall we continue in sin?" Now again he says, "What shall we say then? Is the Law sin?" In the first part of this chapter Paul seems to be saying that law and sin are on a par. If release from sin means release from law, then are they not the same? Paul clarifies this. He says, "Perish the thought!" Paul will now show that the Law is good; it reveals God's will. The difficulty is not with the Law; the difficulty is with us. The flesh is at fault.

Paul becomes very personal in the remainder of this chapter. Notice that he uses the first person pronouns: *I, me* and *myself;* they are used forty–seven times in this section. The experience is the struggle Paul had within himself. He tried to live for God in the power of his new nature. He found it was impossible. The Law revealed to Paul the exceeding sinfulness of sin. The Law was an X-ray of his heart. That is what the Law will do for you if you put it down on your life. The Word of God is called a mirror; it reveals what we are. If you have a spot on your face, the mirror will show it to you, but it can't remove the spot. However, God has a place to remove it:

> There is a fountain filled with blood
> Drawn from Immanuel's veins;
> And sinners, plunged beneath that flood,
> Lose all their guilty stains.

The Law reveals the exceeding sinfulness of sin. The Law is not at fault, but the old Adamic nature is the culprit. The admonition of prohibition contained in the Law makes clear the weakness of the flesh. It shows we are sinners.

Here in California a test was made some time ago. A mirror was put in a very prominent public place, and the test was to see if men or women looked at themselves more. I felt it was an unnecessary test; I could have told them that women looked at themselves more. But unfortunately, the test proved otherwise. We all like to see ourselves. We all like to look in a mirror—except one: the Word of God. We don't like to look in that one because it reveals us as sinners, horrible, lost sinners.

> **For I was alive without the law once: but when the commandment came, sin revived, and I died [Rom. 7:9].**

The Law is a ministry of condemnation. The Law can do nothing but condemn us.

> **And the commandment, which was ordained to life, I found to be unto death [Rom. 7:10].**

Oh, the tragedy of the person who seeks to live by the Law! It does not lead him to life. While it is true that God had said, "This do and thou shalt live" (see Deut. 8:1), the doing of it was the difficulty. The fault was not in the Law, but in the one who thought the Law would bring life an power. It did neither. It merely revealed the weakness, inability, and the sin of mankind. If there had been a law which could have given life, God would have given it (see Gal. 3:21). But life and Christian living do not come by the Law.

Let me illustrate this. A car is a very useful thing. But a car in the hands of an incapable driver can be a danger and a menace. In fact, it can be a death-dealing instrument. The fault is not with the car; the fault is with the driver. The problem is man; he is the culprit.

> **For sin, taking occasion by the commandment, deceived me, and by it slew me [Rom. 7:11].**

Sin is personified again here and is a tempter. Sin tempts every man outside the Garden of Eden relative to himself and God. In the Garden of Eden Satan made man believe that God could not be trusted and that man was able to become god, apart from God. Sin, like a Pied Piper, leads the children of men into believing that they can keep the Law and that God is not needed. This is the false trail that he has been talking about, which leads to death. It was ordained to life, Paul says, and he found it led him to death. Sin at last will kill, for the Law did bring the knowledge of sin, and man is without excuse. Again, the difficulty is not with the Law, but within man.

**Wherefore the law is holy, and the commandment holy, and just, and good [Rom. 7:12].**

The problem is a human problem. Man is the "x" in the equation of life. He is the uncertain one, the one who cannot be trusted.

**Was then that which is good made death unto me? God forbid. But sin, that it might appear sin, working death in mo by that which is good; that sin by the command-ment might become exceeding sinful [Rom. 7:13].**

Is this a strange paradox? Is it a perversion of a good thing? The com-mandment was totally incapable of communicating life. Man must have recourse to help from the outside, because the commandment intensified the awfulness of sin.

**For we know that the law is spiritual: but I am carnal, sold under sin [Rom. 7:14].**

This is Paul's testimony.

"We know" was the general agreement among believers. The Law is spiritual in the sense that it was given by the Holy Spirit and is part of the Word of God. In other words, that is an expression in Scripture. For example, the rock is called spiritual in 1 Corinthians 10:4, for it was produced by the Holy Spirit. Israel in the wilderness had spiritual meat and spiritual drink in this sense—that is, the Spirit of God pro-vided it.

"But I am carnal." This means, "I am in the flesh [Greek *sarkinos*]." It does not mean the meat on the bones of the body. This body of ours is neutral and can be used for that which is either good or bad. It is like the automobile I referred to. Carnality refers to this old human mind and spirit and nature which occupies and uses the flesh so that actually the flesh itself is contaminated with sin. (For example, look upon the face of a baby and then look at the face fifty years later.

Sin has written indelible lines even upon the surface of the body.)
Flesh is inert and has no capabilities or possibilities toward God. It is
dominated by a sinful nature, the ramifications of which reach into
the inmost recesses of the body and mind. The frontal lobe of the brain
is merely an instrument to devise evil. The motor neurons are ready to
spring into evil excesses. The heart of man is desperately wicked. He
wants to do the things that are evil, and the body responds.

Paul describes his pitiful plight as a slave sold to a Simon Legree
taskmaster with a whiplash of evil.

## STRUGGLE OF A SAVED SOUL

**For that which I do I allow not: for what I would, that do
I not; but what I hate, that do I [Rom. 7:15].**

Here we have the conflict of two natures, the old nature and the new
nature. There are definitely two "I's" in this section. The first "I" is
the old nature as he asserts his rights. "For what I would" is what the
new nature wants to do. "That do I not"—the old nature rebels and
won't do it. "But what I hate"—the new nature hates it—"that do I";
the old nature goes right ahead and does it.

Do you have the experience of this struggle in your Christian life?
Do you do something, then hate yourself because you have done it?
And you cry out, "God, oh, how I've failed You!" I think every child of
God has this experience. Paul is speaking of his own experience in
this section. Apparently there were three periods in his life. First he
was a proud Pharisee under the Mosaic system, kidding himself by
bringing the sacrifices and doing other things which he thought
would make him right with God. But the Law was condemning him
all the while. Then the second period began when he met Christ on
the Damascus Road. This proud young Pharisee turned to Christ as
his Savior, but he still felt he could live the Christian life. His new
nature said, "I am now going to live for God!" But he failed and was in
the arena of struggle and failure for a time. I do not know how long it
lasted—probably it was not long. There came a day when there was
victory, but Paul did not win it; Christ did. Paul learned that it was a

mattter of yielding, presenting himself and letting the Spirit of God live the Christian life through him.

**If then I do that which I would not, I consent unto the law that it is good [Rom. 7:16].**

When the old nature breaks the commandment (in this instance it was coveting), then the new nature agrees with the Law that coveting is wrong. Paul was not fighting the Law because he broke it. He was agreeing as a believer that the Law was good.

**Now then it is no more I that do it, but sin that dwelleth in me [Rom. 7:17].**

In other words: It is no longer I (new nature) who am working it out, but sin (the old nature) living in me. You see, Paul still had the old nature.

**For I know that in me (that is, in my flesh,) dwelleth no good thing: for to will is present with me; but how to perform that which is good I find not [Rom. 7:18].**

Paul learned two things in this struggle, and they are something that many of us believers need to learn. "In me (that old nature we have been talking about) dwells no good thing." Have you learned that? Have you found there is no good in you? Oh, how many of us Christians feel that we in the flesh can do something that will please God! Many believers who never find out otherwise become as busy as termites and are having about the same effect in many of our churches. They are busy as bees, but they aren't making any honey! They get on committees, they are chairmen of boards, they try to run the church, and they think they are pleasing God. Although they are busy, they have no vital connection with the person of Christ. His life is not being lived through them. They are attempting to do it in their own strength by the flesh. They haven't learned what Paul learned: "I know that in me (that is, in my flesh,) dwelleth no good thing."

Let me make it personal. Anything that Vernon McGee does in the flesh, God *hates*. God won't have it; God can't use it. When it is of the flesh, it is *no good*. Have you learned that? That is a great lesson. The Lord Jesus said, "That which is born of the flesh is flesh . . ." (John 3:6) (and that is all it will ever be), but "Whosoever is born of God doth not commit sin . . ." (1 John 3:9). My, how wonderful that is! We are given a new nature, and that new nature will not commit sin. I assure you that the new nature won't commit sin. When I sin, it is the old nature. The new nature won't do it; the new nature just *hates* sin. That new nature won't let me sleep at night; it says, "Look, you are wrong. You have to make it right!"

Paul found out something else that is very important for us to learn: "for to will is present with me; but how to perform that which is good I find not." He found there is no *good* in the old nature and there is no *power* in the new nature. The new nature wants to serve God, but the carnal man is at enmity against God; it is not subject to the law of God, neither indeed can be (see Rom. 8:7). But the new nature has no power.

I remember when I started out, oh, I was going to live for God! That's when I fell on my face, and I have never fallen harder than I did then. I thought I could do it myself. But I found there was no power in the new nature. And that is the reason that an evangelist can always get response in a meeting. I'm afraid ninety percent of the decisions that are made in our churches today have been made by Christians who have been living in defeat in their Christian lives. What they are really saying is, "I want to live for God. I want to do better." Often an evangelist in a meeting says, "All of you that want to live for God, put up your hand. All of you today that want to come closer to God, put up your hand. Those of you who want to commit your life to God, come forward." The minute an evangelist says that, he's got me. That is what I want to do. That new nature of mine says, "I sure would like to live for God." But there is no power in it. That is what multitudes of believers fail to recognize. There have been folk who have been coming forward for years, and that's all they have been doing—just coming forward! They never make any progress. Oh, how they need to understand this truth!

> **For the good that I would I do not: but the evil which I would not, that I do [Rom. 7:19].**

Have you experienced this?

> **Now if I do that I would not, it is no more I that do it, but sin that dwelleth in me [Rom. 7:20].**

It is that old nature, my friend, that is causing us trouble.

> **I find then a law, that, when I would do good, evil is present with me [Rom. 7:21].**

When you are attempting to serve God in the Spirit, have you discovered that the old nature is right there to bring evil? Perhaps an evil thought will come into your mind. Every child of God, regardless of his state, must admit that in every act and in every moment evil is present with him. Failure to recognize this will eventually lead to shipwreck in the Christian life.

> **For I delight in the law of God after the inward man [Rom. 7:22].**

"The inward man" is the new nature.

> **But I see another law in my members, warring against the law of my mind, and bringing me into captivity to the law of sin which is in my members [Rom. 7:23].**

You see, you don't get rid of the old nature when you are saved. And yet there is no power in your new nature. "I see a different law" is the enmity of the old nature against God. It causes the child of God who is honest to cry out, as Paul cried:

> **O wretched man that I am! who shall deliver me from the body of this death? [Rom. 7:24].**

This is not an unsaved man who is crying, "O wretched man that I am"; this is a saved man. The word *wretched* carries with it the note of exhaustion because of the struggle. "Who is going to deliver me?" He is helpless. His shoulders are pinned to the floor—he has been wrestled down. Like old Jacob, he has been crippled. He is calling for help from the outside.

**I thank God through Jesus Christ our Lord. So then with the mind I myself serve the law of God; but with the flesh the law of sin [Rom. 7:25].**

"I thank God [who gives deliverance] through Jesus Christ our Lord." This is the answer to Paul's SOS. God has provided deliverance. It introduces chapter 8 in which the deliverance is given in detail. Both salvation and sanctification come through Christ; He has provided everything we need.

> Run, run and do, the Law commands
> But gives me neither feet nor hands.
> Better news the Gospel brings,
> It bids me fly and gives me wings.

# CHAPTER 8

*THEME:* The new man; the new creation; the new body; new purpose

This chapter brings us to the conclusion of sanctification. In fact, it presents three great subjects: sanctification, security, and no separation from God. Here it is powerful sanctification in contrast to powerless sanctification. In this chapter we are going to see God's new provision for our sanctification.

While inadequacy has been my feeling all the way through this epistle, especially here I feel totally incapable of dealing with these great truths. This is such a glorious and wonderful epistle that all we can do is merely stand as Moses did at the burning bush with our feet unshod and our head uncovered, not fully realizing or recognizing the glory and wonder of it all.

Chapter 8 is the high–water mark in Romans. This fact is generally conceded by all interpreters of this great epistle. Spencer said, "If Holy Scripture were a ring and the epistle to the Romans its precious stone, chapter eight would be the sparkling point of the jewel." Godet labeled it, "this incomparable chapter." Someone has added, "We enter this chapter with no condemnation, we close with no separation, and in between all things work together for good to those that love God."

My friend, how could you have it any better than that? We find that joy and peace is to be given to the child of God in this life. He is to live for God in the very presence of sin. Sin is *not* to dictate his life's program. It has already been shown that there is nothing in the justified sinner that can produce this ideal state. We have seen that the new nature has no power and the old nature has no good. Then how is a child of God to live for God? Paul cried out for outside help, "O wretched man that I am! who shall deliver me from the body of this death?" (Rom. 7:24). In other words, who is going to enable me to live for God?

Paul concluded chapter 7 by saying, "I thank God through Jesus Christ our Lord. So then with the mind I myself serve the law of God; but with the flesh the law of sin." Now chapter 8 will give us the modus operandi; that is, the means by which the victory is secured.

This chapter introduces us to the work of the Holy Spirit in sanctification. The Holy Spirit is mentioned nineteen times in this chapter. Before chapter 8 there were only two casual references (see Rom. 5:5; 7:6). In this epistle we see the work of the Blessed Trinity:

God the Father in creation (Rom. 1:1—3:20)
God the Son in salvation (Rom. 3:21—7:25)
God the Holy Spirit in sanctification (Rom. 8:1–39)

Now here in chapter 8 we see the Holy Spirit and real sanctification. A life that is pleasing to God must be lived in the power of the Holy Spirit. As Paul said to the Ephesian believers, "And be not drunk with wine, wherein is excess; but be filled with the Spirit" (Eph. 5:18). Sanctification is the work of the Holy Spirit in the regenerated life of a believer, delivering the believer from the power of sin—even in the very presence of sin—and performing all God's will in the life of the believer.

Godet labels the first eleven verses "The Victory of the Holy Spirit over Sin and Death."

**There is therefore now no condemnation to them which are in Christ Jesus, who walk not after the flesh, but after the Spirit [Rom. 8:1].**

"Who walk not after the flesh, but after the Spirit" does not really belong in this verse. Apparently some scribe picked it up from verse 4 where it belongs. The literal rendering is: "Therefore now, not one condemnation." This is the inspired statement that, in spite of the failure that Paul experienced in chapter 7, he did not lose his salvation. There is no condemnation to those who are in Christ Jesus. However, he wasn't enjoying the Christian life—he was a failure, and he was a wretched man. God wanted him to have joy in his life. Now how is he to have this? Notice the next verse.

> **For the law of the Spirit of life in Christ Jesus hath made me free from the law of sin and death [Rom. 8:2].**

This is a very important statement. This little word *for* occurs seventeen times in this chapter. Because it is the cement that holds the chapter together, it is a word that requires real mental effort. We need to follow the logic of the apostle Paul. One of the great expositors of Romans said that if you do not find Paul logical, you are not following him aright.

"The law of the Spirit" means not only a principle of law, but also the authority which is exercised by the Spirit.

"The Spirit of life" means the Holy Spirit who brings life because He essentially is life. He is the Spirit of life.

"In Christ Jesus" means that the Holy Spirit is in complete union with Christ Jesus. Because the believer shares the life of Christ, He liberates the believers.

"The law of sin and death" is the authority that sin had over our old nature, ending in complete severance of fellowship with God. That new nature could not break the shackles at all. Only the coming of a higher authority and power could accomplish this, namely the Holy Spirit. The Holy Spirit operates upon the new nature, which is vitally joined to the life of Christ. The man in Romans 7, who was joined to the body of the dead, is now joined to the living Christ also.

> **For what the law could not do, in that it was weak through the flesh, God sending his own Son in the likeness of sinful flesh, and for sin, condemned sin in the flesh:**
>
> **That the righteousness of the law might be fulfilled in us, who walk not after the flesh, but after the Spirit [Rom. 8:3–4].**

We have here the whole crux of the matter. Let me give my translation, which may bring out several things we need to understand. "For the thing impossible for the Law in which it was powerless through the flesh, God, having sent His own Son in the likeness of the flesh of sin, and in regard to sin, He condemned the sin in the flesh; in order that the justification (the righteous result) of the Law might be fulfilled in us, who walk not according to flesh but according to Spirit."

It was impossible for the Law to produce righteousness in man. This is not the fault of the Law. The fault lay in man and the sin in his flesh. The Law was totally incapable of producing any good thing in man. Paul could say, "For I know that in me (that is, in my flesh,) dwelleth no good thing" (Rom. 7:18). And friend, that is Scripture, and that is accurate. Man is totally depraved. That doesn't mean only the man across the street or down in the next block from you, nor does it mean only some person who is living in sin; it means you and it means me. The Holy Spirit is now able to do the impossible. The Holy Spirit can produce a holy life in the weak and sinful flesh. Let me illustrate this truth by using a very homely incident. Suppose a housewife puts a roast in the oven right after breakfast because she is going to serve it for the noon meal. The telephone rings. It is Mrs. Joe Dokes on the phone. Mrs. Dokes begins with "Have you heard?" Well, the housewife hasn't heard, but she would like to; so she pulls up a chair. (Someone has defined a woman as one who draws up a chair when answering a telephone.) Mrs. Dokes has a lot to tell, and about an hour goes by. Finally our good housewife says, "Oh, Mrs. Dokes, you'll have to excuse me. I smell the roast—its burning!" She hangs up the phone, rushes to the kitchen, and opens the oven. Then she gets a fork and puts it down in the roast to lift it up, but it won't hold. She can't lift it out. She tries again, closer to the bone, but still it won't hold. So she gets a spatula. She puts the spatula under the roast and lifts it out. You see, what the fork could not do, in that it was weak through the flesh, the spatula is able to do. Now, there is nothing wrong with the fork—it was a good fork. But it couldn't hold the flesh because something was wrong with the flesh—it was overcooked. The spatula does what the fork could not do.

The Law is like the fork in that it was weak through the flesh. It just won't lift us up; it *can't* lift us up. But a new principle is introduced: the Holy Spirit. What the Law could not do, the Holy Spirit is able to do. Therefore, you and I are to live the Christian life on this new principle. We are not to try to lift ourselves up by our own bootstraps. We'll never make it that way, my friend. We make resolutions and say, "I'm going to do better"—all of us have said that. But did we ever do better? Didn't we do the same old things?

God is able to do this new impossible thing by sending His very own Son, His own nature in the likeness of sinful flesh. Christ had the same kind of flesh that we have, apart from sin. Notice how the writer to the Hebrews puts it: "Forasmuch then as the children are partakers of flesh and blood, he also himself likewise took part of the same; that through death he might destroy him that had the power of death, that is, the devil . . . . For verily he took not on him the nature of angels; but he took on him the seed of Abraham. Wherefore in all things it behoved him to be made like unto his brethren, that he might be a merciful and faithful high priest in things pertaining to God, to make reconciliation for the sins of the people" (Heb. 2:14, 16–17). Also he says, "For such an high priest became us, who is holy, harmless, undefiled, separate from sinners, and made higher than the heavens" (Heb. 7:26). Then he says, "Wherefore when he cometh into the world, he saith, Sacrifice and offering thou wouldest not, but a body hast thou prepared me" (Heb. 10:5).

This was God's way of getting at the roots of sin in our bodies, minds, and spirits. He could condemn and execute sinful flesh on the Cross so that is had no more rights in human beings. God was able to deal with sin itself—Christ was identified with us—what condescension! Sin has been condemned in these bodies of ours. It has not been removed, in spite of the belief of some very sincere people. These bodies are to be redeemed—". . . raised a spiritual body . . ." (1 Cor. 15:44). Today, the Holy Spirit is the Deliverer from sin in the body. A great many people think it would be wonderful if Christ would come and take us out of this world of sin—and that would be wonderful. I wish He would come right now. However, there is something even more wonderful than that. It is this: He enables you and me to live the Christian life right where we are today in this old world of sin. That is more wonderful. Our Lord Jesus said in His high priestly prayer, "I pray not that thou shouldest take them out of the world, but that thou shouldest keep them from the evil" (John 17:15). Down here is where the victory is.

"That the righteousness of the law might be fulfilled"—this is the passive voice. It means that the Holy Spirit produces a life of obedience which the Law commanded but could not produce. The Holy Spirit furnishes the power; the decision is ours.

The next verse introduces us to a new struggle. It is not for us to do the fighting. Now it is the Holy Spirit versus the flesh.

> **For they that are after the flesh do mind the things of the flesh; but they that are after the Spirit the things of the Spirit [Rom. 8:5].**

"Do mind the things of the flesh." When I was holding a meeting in Middle Tennessee after I was first ordained, I was invited to dinner in a lovely country home. The housewife had prepared some wonderful fried chicken. When we were already sitting at the table, she went out to call her little boy again. After she'd called him several times, she came in and said, "That young'un won't *mind* me." And what she meant was, "That young one will not obey me." Paul, you see, sounds like a good Southerner because he uses this word, "they *mind* the things of the flesh." We have seen that before in the sixth chapter of Romans. My friend, if you live habitually in the flesh and obey the things of the flesh, and the new nature doesn't rebuke you, you must not have a new nature—because "they that are after the Spirit [mind] the things of the Spirit." A believer has been given a new nature, and now he can yield himself to the new nature. And this is an act of the will. This is the new struggle that's brought to our attention. "The flesh" describes the natural man. The Lord Jesus said, "that which is born of the flesh is flesh"—it will always be flesh. God has no program to change the flesh. Rather He brings in something new: "and that which is born of the Spirit is spirit" (John 3:6).

A new struggle is brought to our attention. It is no longer the new nature or the believer striving for mastery over sin in the body; it is the Holy Spirit striving against the old nature. The little boy coming home from school was being beaten up by a big bully. He was on the bottom, and the big bully was pounding him very heavily. Then he looked up from his defeated position on the bottom, and he saw his big brother coming. The big brother took care of the bully while the little fellow crawled up on a stump and rubbed his bruises. The believer has the Holy Spirit to deal with the flesh, that big bully. I learned a long time ago that I can't overcome it. So I have to turn it over to somebody who can. The Holy Spirit indwells believers. He wants to do that for us, and He can!

"They that are after the flesh" describes the natural man. Paul paints his picture in Ephesians 2:1–3. "And you hath he quickened, who were dead in trespasses and sins: wherein in time past ye walked according to the course of this world, according to the prince of the power of the air, the spirit that now worketh in the children of disobedience: among whom also we all had our conversation in times past in the lusts of our flesh, fulfilling the desires of the flesh and of the mind; and were by nature the children of wrath, even as others." This was the condition of all of us until we were saved.

And the "flesh" includes the mind. "And you, that were sometime alienated and enemies in your mind by wicked works, yet now hath he reconciled" (Col. 1:21). It includes the total personality which is completely alienated from God.

The natural man strives and even sets his heart upon the things of the flesh. Here is his diet: "Now the works of the flesh are manifest, which are these; adultery, fornication, uncleanness, lasciviousness, idolatry, witchcraft, hatred, variance, emulations, wrath, strife, seditions, heresies, envyings, murders, drunkenness, revellings, and such like: of the which I tell you before, as I have told you in time past, that they which do such things shall not inherit the kingdom of God" (Gal. 5:19–21). It is an ugly brood!

In Colossians Paul says: "But now ye also put off all these; anger, wrath, malice, blasphemy, filthy communication out of your mouth. Lie not one to another, seeing that ye have put off the old man with his deeds" (Col. 3:8–9). The Lord Jesus said: "For out of the heart proceed evil thoughts, murders, adulteries, fornications, thefts, false witness, blasphemies" (Matt. 15:19).

It is humiliating but true that the child of God retains this old Adamic nature. It means defeat and death to live by the flesh. No child of God can be happy in living for the things of the flesh. The prodigal son may get into the pigpen, but he will never be content to stay there. He is bound to say, "I will arise and go to my father."

"They that are after the Spirit" are born again, regenerated and indwelt by the Spirit of God. They love the things of Christ. "If ye then be risen with Christ, seek those things which are above, where Christ sitteth on the right hand of God. Set your affection on things above, not on things on the earth" (Col. 3:1–2). And Paul says, "Put on therefore, as the elect of God, holy and beloved, bowels of mercies, kindness, humbleness of mind, meekness, longsuffering" (Col. 3:12). These are just some of the things for which the child of God longs. You and I cannot do these things by effort. It is only as we let the Spirit of God work in our lives that they will appear.

Here is another great principle.

> **For to be carnally minded is death; but to be spiritually minded is life and peace [Rom. 8:6].**

"For to be carnally minded" means that you are separated from fellowship with God and that flesh is death here and now. The Spirit who indwells the believer brings life and peace. When we sin, we are to come to Him in confession and let Him wash us. This restores us to fellowship.

The "life" He offers speaks of full satisfaction and the exercise of one's total abilities. Oh, to live life at its fullest and best! Many people think they are really living today, but it is a shoddy substitute for the life God wants to provide.

"Peace" means the experience of tranquility and well-being regarding the present and future. Oh, my beloved, how you and I need to get into that territory!

There is one thing for sure: if you are living in the flesh, and you are a child of God, you are *not* having fellowship with God. You *can't*. The Lord Jesus in the Upper Room said to Simon Peter, ". . . If I wash thee not, thou hast no part with me" (John 13:8). Now, my friend, He meant that. He will not fellowship with you or with me if we are committing sin and are continuing to live in the flesh. "Well," somebody says, "what are we to do?" Do what Simon Peter had to do—he stuck out his feet and let the Lord wash them. And you and I need to go to Him in confession. First John 1:9 tells us, "If we confess our sins." Who is "we"? We Christians. "He is faithful and just . . ." when He does it, because it will take the blood of Christ, my friend. You and I do not know how wicked the old nature is. And we need to go to Him for cleansing.

The English poet, John Donne, using the mythological story of the labors of Hercules—where that strongman of the ancient world was confronted with the task of cleaning out the Augean stables—illustrates this important truth. Though Hercules was able to perform the task, Donne shows that man cannot clean the much greater filth of the human heart. He writes:

> Lord I confess that Thou alone are able
> To purify this Augean stable.
> Be the seas water, and all the land soap
> Yet if Thy blood not wash me—there's no hope.

The blood of Jesus Christ, God's Son, keeps on cleansing us from all sin (see 1 John 1:7). This old nature is totally depraved. God has no plan to redeem it. He gives us a new nature. And you and I can't live for God in that old nature. If you continue to live in that old nature, you must not be a child of God. Somebody says, "Then if a child of God sins, what's the difference between him and the lost man?" The difference is simply this: when the lost man goes out at night and paints the town red, he comes back and says, "I'll get a bigger brush and a bigger bucket of paint next time; wow, I want to live it up!" While the child of God, if he does a thing like that, will cry out to God, "Oh, God, I hate myself for what I've done!" And this idea today that you can somehow train your old nature, and live in it, is false.

That's the thing that leads to legalism. Legalists—well, I call them Priscilla Goodbodies and Goody-goody-gumdrops, those sweet lovely people who are trying to control the flesh—they are so pious! I want to tell you, they are the worst gossips you have ever met.

Dr. Newell has put down some very interesting statements which I would like to pass on to you. "To hope to do better is to fail to see yourself in Christ only." You say, "I hope to do better." You *know* you're not. You need to see yourself in Christ today and realize that only the Spirit of God moving through you can accomplish this. And then Newell says again, "To be disappointed with yourself means you believed in yourself." Somebody says, "Oh, I'm so disappointed in myself." Well, you had better be disappointed in yourself. You know no good thing is going to come out of the flesh, friend. Stop believing in yourself, and believe that the Spirit of God today can enable you through the new nature to live for God. Also Newell says, "To be discouraged is unbelief." Somebody says, "Oh, I'm so discouraged." My friend, that means you don't believe God. God has a purpose and a plan, a blessing for you. And you need to lay hold of it. Here is another statement: "To be proud is to be blind." We have no standing before God in ourselves. Oh, my friend, see yourself as God sees you. Here is the final gem: "The lack of divine blessing comes from unbelief, not a failure of devotion." I am so sick and weary of these super-duper pious, "dedicated" Christians who talk about their devotion. My friend, the lack of divine blessing comes because we do not *believe* God. It is not because of a lack of devotion. Oh, to believe God today! Now, real devotion arises not from man's will to show it, but from the discovery that blessing has been received from God while we were yet unworthy and undevoted. Nothing I get from God has come through my devotion. I haven't anything to offer Him. It comes because of His marvelous grace. And I've seen these folk who preach "devotion" troop down to dedicate their lives in services. I got so sick and tired of seeing that same crowd come down—and you could not trust them, my friend. They were liars. They were dishonest. They were gossips, and they would crucify you. May I say to you, you do not need to dedicate yourself. What you need today is to *believe* God can do something and you can't do anything. Now, somebody says, "That's pretty strong." I hope that it is. I intend for it to be that way, because Paul is making it very clear here. The carnal mind is enmity against God.

**Because the carnal mind is enmity against God: for it is not subject to the law of God, neither indeed can be.**

**So then they that are in the flesh cannot please God [Rom. 8:7–8].**

This verse reveals how hopelessly incorrigible and utterly destitute the flesh really is. It is a spiritual anarchist. This demolishes any theory that there is a divine spark in man and that somehow he has a secret bent toward God. The truth is that man is the enemy of God. He is not only dead in trespasses and sins but active in rebellion against God. Man will even become religious in order to stay away from the living and true God and the person of Jesus Christ. Man in his natural condition, if taken to heaven, would start a revolution, and he would have a protest meeting going on before the sun went down! Jacob, in his natural condition, engaged in a wrestling match. He did not seek it, but he fought back when God wrestled with him. It wasn't until he yielded that he won, my friend.

Anything that the flesh produces is not acceptable to God. The so-called good work, the civilization, the culture, and man's vaunted progress are all a stench in the nostrils of God. The religious works of church people done in the lukewarmness of the flesh make Christ sick to His stomach (see Rev. 3:15–16).

I wonder if we are willing to accept God's estimation of our human boasting. This is a terrible picture of man; but it is accurate. Yet there is deliverance in the Spirit of God. Are you willing, my friend, to turn it over to the Holy Spirit and quit trusting that weak, sinful nature that you have? That is the question.

**But ye are not in the flesh, but in the Spirit, if so be that the Spirit of God dwell in you. Now if any man have not the Spirit of Christ, he is none of his [Rom. 8:9].**

This first "if" is not casting a doubt over the Roman believers' salvation. They are saved. Let me give you a literal translation: "But you are not in the flesh, but in the Spirit *since* the Spirit of God really dwells in you." That is the real test. But if anyone has "not the Spirit of Christ, he is none of his." The true mark of a born-again believer and a genuine Christian is that he is indwelt by the Spirit of God. Even Paul could say to the carnal Corinthians: "What? know ye not that your body is the temple of the Holy Ghost which is in you, which ye have of God, and ye are not your own?" (1 Cor. 6:19). When Paul went to Ephesus the first time, he missed something; he missed the distinguishing mark of the believer. So he asked, "Did you receive the Holy Spirit when you believed?" They didn't even know what he was talking about. So he asked them, ". . . Unto what then were ye baptized? And they said, Unto John's baptism" (Acts 19:3). Well, John's baptism was unto repentance; it was not to faith in Jesus Christ. So he preached Christ to them. Then they received Him and were baptized in His name (see Acts 19:5). A believer is a new creation. Do you love Him? Do you want to serve Him? Are these things uppermost in your mind and heart? Or are you in rebellion against God?

> **And if Christ be in you, the body is dead because of sin; but the spirit is life because of righteousness [Rom. 8:10].**

In other words: Now if Christ be in you, the body indeed is dead on account of sin; but the Spirit is life because of righteousness. He is saying here that you and I are in Christ, and since we are in Him, when He died, we died. And we are to reckon on this, as we have already been told. Also we are to yield, that is, *present* our bodies to Him. Don't say you can't do this—that is not the language of a believer. Paul could say, "I am crucified with Christ: nevertheless I live; yet not I, but Christ liveth in me: and the life which I now live in the flesh I live by the faith of the Son of God, who loved me, and gave himself for me" (Gal. 2:20).

If you today are not conscious of the presence of the Spirit of God in your life and if you do not have a desire to serve God, then it would be well to do as Paul suggests, "Examine yourselves, whether ye be in the faith; prove your own selves. Know ye not your own selves, how that Jesus Christ is in you, except ye be reprobates?" (2 Cor. 13:5). The Lord wants us to *know* that we are in Christ. "To whom God would make known what is the riches of the glory of this mystery among the Gentiles; which is Christ in you, the hope of glory" (Col. 1:27).

If you are not sure that Christ is in you, He extends this invitation: "Behold, I stand at the door, and knock: if any man hear my voice, and open the door, I will come in to him, and will sup with him, and he with me" (Rev. 3:20). Is your door open? Has He come into you? My friend, the body has been put in the place of death. This is something the child of God should reckon on. And he should turn over his life to the Spirit of God, saying very definitely, "I cannot do it, Lord, but You can do it through me."

> **But if the Spirit of him that raised up Jesus from the dead dwell in you, he that raised up Christ from the dead shall also quicken your mortal bodies by his Spirit that dwelleth in you [Rom. 8:11].**

These bodies that you and I have will be put in the grave one of these days, if the Lord tarries. However, the indwelling Holy Spirit is our assurance that our bodies will be raised from the dead (2 Cor. 5:1–4). Because Christ was raised from the dead, we shall be raised from the dead. The Holy Spirit will deliver us from the "body of his death"— this old nature.

> **Therefore, brethren, we are debtors, not to the flesh, to live after the flesh [Rom. 8:12].**

In other words, we are not to live according to the flesh. God created man body, mind, and spirit. When man sinned, his spirit died to God. Remember that God warned, "But of the tree of the knowledge of good and evil, thou shalt not eat of it: for in the day that thou eatest thereof thou shalt surely die" (Gen. 2:17). After Adam ate of the fruit, he lived several hundred years—physically; but spiritually he died immediately. Man was turned upside down. The body, the old nature, the flesh became dominant. Today man is dead spiritually. Regeneration means that you are turned right side up, that you are born again spiritually, and that you have a nature which wants to serve God.

Oh, my friend, to stay close to Christ is the important thing. You can be active in Christian work, as active as a termite, yet Christ can be in outer space as far as you are concerned. The natural man says he owes it to his flesh to satisfy it. He may rationalize his dishonesty by saying, "A man has to eat." A movie star has said, "I live for sex, and I have to have my needs met." We hear this today on every hand. Satisfying the old nature has plunged our nation into the grossest immorality! But God says that we as believers are not debtors to the flesh. My friend, the flesh—and we all have it—is a low-down, dirty rascal. And we don't owe it anything.

> **For if ye live after the flesh, ye shall die: but if ye through the Spirit do mortify the deeds of the body, ye shall live [Rom. 8:13].**

"For if ye live after the flesh, ye shall die"—die to God. That is, you have no fellowship with Him. I am not talking about a theory; if you are a child of God, you know this from experience. If you are a child of God and you have unconfessed sin in your life, do you *want* to go to church? Do you *want* to read your Bible? Do you *want* to pray? Of course you don't. You are separated from God.

"But if ye through the Spirit"—you can't do it yourself—"do mortify the deeds of the body, ye shall live." Let's be practical now. What is your problem today? Liquor? Drugs? Sex? You may say, "I don't have those problems!" Then how about your thought-life? How about your tongue? Do you gossip? Do you tell the truth? Whatever your problem is, why don't you confess it to God, then turn it over to the Holy Spirit? My friend, if you deal with it in reality, you won't need to crawl up on the psychiatrist's couch. He won't help you. He can shift your guilt complex to another area, but he can't get rid of it. Only Christ can remove it; He is in that business. He says, "Come unto me,

all ye that labour and are heavy laden, and I will rest you" so that you
will know what it is to have sins forgiven (see Matt. 11:28).

## THE NEW MAN

We come now to a new section concerning the new nature of man.

> **For as many as are led by the Spirit of God, they are the
> sons of God [Rom. 8:14].**

That makes sense, doesn't it? God does not drive His sheep; He leads
them. When our Lord told of the safety and security of the sheep, He
made it clear that they were not forced into the will of His hand and
that of the Father. He said, "My sheep hear my voice, and I know them
[and I drive them out! Oh, no] and they follow me" (John 10:27). They
are the ones who are safe and secure; they follow Him. They are led by
the Spirit of God. They hear His voice because they have a new nature,
and they follow Him.

I have been preaching the Word of God for a long time. I have found
that those who are His sheep will hear His voice. The others—they
hated me and wanted to get rid of me. Why? They were not His sheep.
The Lord Jesus said, "If the world hate you, ye know that it hated me
before it hated you" (John 15:18). A young pastor came to me and
said, "I'm having all kinds of trouble!" I asked, "Who is giving you
trouble?" He said, "My church officers and my Sunday school teach-
ers." So I asked him what he had been doing. He said, "Well, I've been
preaching the Bible, following your Thru the Bible method." I said to
him, "Well, thank God. You will find that a lot of your folk are not
really His sheep." Friend, His sheep will follow Him—they have to
because they are His, you see. That's what Paul is saying here.

> **For ye have not received the spirit of bondage again to
> fear; but ye have received the Spirit of adoption,
> whereby we cry, Abba, Father [Rom. 8:15].**

"Ye have not received the spirit of bondage again to fear"—there is not
the spirit of fear within you, wondering about your spiritual condi-

tion, unhappy, and despondent. Instead, you are filled with joy because you are His child. And the Spirit of God wells up within you, saying, "Abba, Father."

The word *Abba* is an untranslated Aramaic word. The translators of the first English Bibles, who had great reverence for the Word of God, who believed it was indeed the Word of God, would not translate it. *Abba* is a very personal word that could be translated "My Daddy." We don't use this word in reference to God because of the danger of becoming overly familiar with Him. But it expresses a heartcry, especially in times of trouble.

**The Spirit itself beareth witness with our spirit, that we are the children of God [Rom. 8:16].**

I found this true the first time I went to the hospital for cancer surgery. I turned my face to the wall, like old Hezekiah did, and said, "Lord, I've been in this hospital many times. I've patted the hands of folk and had prayer with them, and told them, 'Oh, you trust the Lord; He will see you through.' Lord, I have told *them* that, but this is the first time *I've* been in here. Now I want to know whether it is true or not. I want You to make it real to me. If You are my Father, I want to *know* it. And, my friend, He made it real. At a time like that the Spirit of God cries out, "Abba, Father"—it just wells up within you. How sweet it is to trust Him, turn yourself over to Him.

**And if children, then heirs; heirs of God, and joint-heirs with Christ; if so be that we suffer with him, that we may be also glorified together [Rom. 8:17].**

"If so be" assures the fact that the child of God will suffer with Him. I believe it could be translated "*since* we suffer with Him." I don't think the "if" is as important as some folk make it out to be.

My friend, what are you enduring for Him today? Whatever it is, Paul makes it clear that it is just a light thing we are going through now. But there is a weighty thing, an "eternal weight of glory" that is coming someday. In eternity we will wish that we had suffered a little more for Him, because that is the way He schools and trains us. "For whom the Lord loveth he chasteneth, and scourgeth every son whom he receiveth" (Heb. 12:6).

## THE NEW CREATION

This brings us to a new division in this eighth chapter of Romans.

Not only the bodies of believers are to be redeemed, but we're going to find out that this entire physical universe, this earth on which you and I live, is to be redeemed. That is the purpose of God. In fact we're trading in this old earth for a new earth, a new model, brand new, wherein there will be no sin. No curse of sin will ever come upon it again. That is something that is quite wonderful. Someone said to me not long ago, "I believe that healing is in the Atonement." I think I shocked the person when I said, "I believe that too. Not only is healing in the Atonement, but a new body is in the Atonement, and a new world is in the atonement of Christ. But we don't have it yet." The political parties and the United Nations have been trying to bring in a new world for years, but we certainly do not have these yet. But Christ is going to bring it in someday through His redemption. And then I'm going to get a new body. I'm looking forward to that. This one I've got is wearing out, and I want to trade it in for a new one. And that's coming. And healing—I'll grant that it is in the Atonement, but I don't have all of that yet. I still have cancer.

> **For I reckon that the sufferings of this present time are not worthy to be compared with the glory which shall be revealed in us [Rom. 8:18].**

"I reckon" means that Paul calculates, counts upon, both the debit and credit side of the ledger of life.

"The sufferings of this present time" are the common lot of all believers. This generation, which is enjoying more creature comforts than any other in history, frowns upon this statement, but even present-day Christians cannot escape suffering.

**For the earnest expectation of the creature waiteth for the manifestation of the sons of God [Rom. 8:19].**

Let me give my translation of this verse: For the creation, watching with outstretched head (head erect), is waiting (sighing) for the revelation of the sons of God.

The world is not waiting for the sunrise of evolution's pipe dream. The pipe dream of evolution will never come true. However, creation is waiting "for the manifestation of the sons of God." Creation is like a veiled statue today. When the sons of God have removed the outward covering of this flesh, creation also will be unveiled. What a glorious day that will be!

**For the creature was made subject to vanity, not willingly, but by reason of him who hath subjected the same in hope [Rom. 8:20].**

"For the creation was subjected to vanity"—*vanity* means "failure, decay, something that is perishable."

"Not willingly" means not of its own will, but because of Him who subjected it on the basis of hope. King Solomon, who was quite a pessimist, by the way, wrote: "All the rivers run into the sea; yet the sea is not full; unto the place from whence the rivers come, thither they return again" (Eccl. 1:7). There is a weary round of repetition. The rivers run into the sea, and the Lord has quite a hydraulic pump that pumps the water right out of the ocean, and with His good transportation system, the wind moves the clouds across the dry land, and here comes the rain again. It fills the rivers, and the rivers run into the sea. There is a monotony about nature; you see it on every hand. Nature is waiting for the promised manifestation, the unveiling.

"Creation was subjected to vanity" because God made it that way. The curse of sin came upon man in Adam's disobedience, but the physical world also came under the curse. Remember that God said to Adam, "Thorns also and thistles shall it bring forth to thee; and thou shalt eat the herb of the field; In the sweat of thy face shalt thou eat bread . . ." (Gen. 3:18–19). I enjoy going out to the Hawaiian Islands; I know of no place quite as delightful. Yet on a golf course in that "paradise" I found—of all things—thorns! I knocked a ball out in the rough there, out in the lava, and I have never seen as many thorns as were there. I have a pair of shoes that have thorns in them to this good day—I can't get them all out. Even in that paradise there are thorns. There is a curse on creation.

> **Because the creature itself also shall be delivered from the bondage of corruption into the glorious liberty of the children of God [Rom. 8:21].**

Man has a dying body. As someone has said, "The moment He gives us life, He begins to take it away from us." And there is death and decay yonder in nature. Go out in the beautiful forest, and there you see a tree lying dead, corrupt, rotting. That's nature. And you catch the stench of the decaying bodies of dead animals.

> **For we know that the whole creation groaneth and travaileth in pain together until now [Rom. 8:22].**

Browning in his *Pippa Passes* writes:

> God's in His Heaven—
> All's right with the world.

The Christian knows that that is not true. God is in His heaven all right, but all is not right with the world. The Word of God is more realistic: "How do the beasts groan! the herds of cattle are perplexed, because they have no pasture; yea, the flocks of sheep are made desolate" (Joel 1:18).

   Some have called our attention to the fact that nature sings in a minor key. The wind blowing through the pine trees on a mountainside and the breaking of the surf on some lonely shore—both emit the same sob. The music of trees has been recorded, and it is doleful. The startled cry of some frightened animal or bird pierces the night air and chills the blood. Surely nature bears audible testimony to the accuracy of Scipture. Godet quotes Schelling in this connection, "Nature, with its melancholy chorus, resembles a bride who, at the very moment when she is fully attired for the marriage, saw the bridegroom die. She still stands with her fresh crown and in her bridal dress but her eyes are full of tears."

It is accurate to say that "nature is groaning."

## THE NEW BODY

**And not only they, but ourselves also, which have the firstfruits of the Spirit, even we ourselves groan within ourselves, waiting for the adoption, to wit, the redemption of our body [Rom. 8:23].**

Not only does nature groan, but the believer is in harmony with nature. This verse is devastating to those who propose the theory that the mark of a Christian is a perennially smiling face. They contend that a Christian should be a cross between a Cheshire cat and a house-to-house salesman. A Christian should grin—at all times. Smile your troubles away is good for Rotary, but it is not the Christian method.

We groan within these bodies. Some years ago when I began to move into middle age, I would come down the steps in the morning groaning because my knees were hurting. My wife told me I ought not to groan! I told her it is scriptural to groan. Paul says, "For in this we groan, earnestly desiring to be clothed upon with our house which is from heaven" (2 Cor. 5:2). Also the psalmist wrote, "I am weary with my groaning; all the night make I my bed to swim; I water my couch with my tears" (Ps. 6:6). Our Lord Jesus did some weeping also. Although I believe He was a joyful person, there were times when He wept. In these bodies we groan.

**For we are saved by hope: but hope that is seen is not hope: for what a man seeth, why doth he yet hope for? [Rom. 8:24].**

"We are saved by hope" speaks of the work of Christ for us on the Cross and our faith in Him. But that is not all. We have a redeemed body coming up in the future.

> **But if we hope for that we see not, then do we with patience wait for it [Rom. 8:25].**

You see, faith, hope, and love are the vital parts of the believer's life. There would be no hope if all were realized. Someday hope will pass away in realization. In fact, both faith and hope will pass away in the glory which shall be revealed in us. Only love abides.

> **Likewise the Spirit also helpeth our infirmities: for we know not what we should pray for as we ought: but the Spirit itself maketh intercession for us with groanings which cannot be uttered [Rom. 8:26].**

Years ago when the late Dr. A. C. Gaebelein was speaking, a very enthusiastic member of the congregation kept interrupting with loud amens. That annoyed Dr. Gaebelein. Finally, he told him, "Brother, the Scripture says that the Spirit maketh intercession for us with groanings which cannot be uttered—so don't you utter them if it's the Spirit of God." We didn't even know how we ought to pray; but the Spirit of God will make intercession with groanings which cannot be uttered.

Have you gone to God sometimes in prayer when you actually did not know what to pray for? All you could do was just go to Him and say, "Father." You could not ask anything because you didn't know what to ask for. At times like this the Spirit "helpeth our infirmities." How wonderful that is!

> **And he that searcheth the hearts knoweth what is the mind of the Spirit, because he maketh intercession for the saints according to the will of God [Rom. 8:27].**

Now, if I go to God in prayer and say, "Look, Lord, I want You to do it this way," that's the way I usually do it, and I may not get the answer the way I prayed. But it's wonderful sometimes to go to the Lord and say, "Lord, I don't know what to ask for. I don't know what to say. But I'm coming to You as Your child. And I want Your *will* done." And the Sprit of God then will make intercession for us according to the will of God. My, again, how wonderful that is!

## NEW PURPOSE

We come now to the new purpose of God. If Romans is the greatest book of the Bible, and chapter 8 is the high-water mark, then verse 28 is the pinnacle. God's purpose guarantees the salvation of sinners, and the next three verses give the "ascending process of salvation," as William Sanday calls it.

**And we know that all things work together for good to them that love God, to them who are the called according to his purpose [Rom. 8:28].**

I have translated it this way: But we know (with divine knowledge) that for those who love God, all things are working together for good, even to them who are called-ones according to His purpose.

The late Dr. Reuben A. Torrey (I had the privilege of being pastor for twenty-one years of the church that he founded) was a great man of God, greatly abused and misunderstood. He knew the meaning of this verse, and he called it a soft pillow for a tired heart. Many of us have pillowed our heads on Romans 8:28. We know the whole creation is groaning, but we also know something else: all things are working together for good—even the groanings.

"We know" is used five times in Romans, and "know" is used thirteen times. It refers to that which is the common knowledge of the Christian, that is, that which the Holy Spirit makes real. "Knowledge puffeth up, but love edifieth" (see 1 Cor. 8:1), and this is the knowledge that only the Spirit of God can make real to our hearts. Charles Spurgeon used to say, "I do not need anyone to tell me how honey tastes; I *know.*" And I can say, my friend, that I *know* God loves me. I don't need to argue that point; I *know* it.

"For those who love God" is the fraternity pin of the believer. "For in Jesus Christ neither circumcision availeth any thing, nor uncircumcision [that is, there is no badge]; but faith which worketh by love" (Gal. 5:6). Love is the mark. The apostle John put it like this: "Herein is love, not that we loved God, but that he loved us, and sent his Son to be the propitiation [the mercy seat] for our sins. Beloved, if God so loved us, we ought also to love one another. No man hath seen God at any time. If we love one another, God dwelleth in us, and his love is perfected in us. Hereby know we that we dwell in him, and he in us, because he hath given us of his Spirit. And we have seen and do testify that the Father sent the Son to be the Saviour of the world. Whosoever shall confess that Jesus is the Son of God, God dwelleth in him, and he in God. And we have known and believed the love that God hath to us. God is love; and he that dwelleth in love dwelleth in God, and God in him" (1 John 4:10–16). My friend, you are going to have trouble believing that God loves you, and you will have difficulty loving God, if you are hating other Christians. "We love him, because first loved us" (1 John 4:19). And the apostle Peter said: "Whom having not seen, ye love; in whom, though now ye see him not, yet believing, ye rejoice with joy unspeakable and full of glory" (1 Pet. 1:8). The thing that will bring joy and brightness into your life is the sincere love of God.

"All things"—good and bad; bright and dark; sweet and bitter; easy and hard; happy and sad; prosperity and poverty; health and sickness; calm and storm; comfort and suffering; life and death.

"Are working together for good" is causative and means that God is working all things—there are no accidents. You remember that Joseph could look back over his life, a life that had been filled with vicissitudes, disappointments, and sufferings, yet he could say to his brethren—who were responsible for his misfortune—". . . ye thought evil against me; but God meant it unto good . . ." (Gen. 50:20). And I am confident that we as children of God will be able to look back over our lives someday, and say, "All of this worked out for good." Job could say, "Though he slay me, yet will I trust in him . . ." (Job 13:15).

That is the kind of faith in God we need, friend. We know that He is going to make things work out for good because He's the One who is motivating it. He's the One who is energizing it.

However, we often cry out, as Jeremiah did, "Why did you let me see trouble?" (see Jer. 11:14). It was during the San Francisco earthquake many years ago that a saint of God walked out into the scene of destruction and debris and actually smiled. A friend asked her, "How can you smile at a time like this?" Her reply was, "I rejoice that I have a God who can shake the world!" How wonderful to be able to face life—and death—unafraid. I think of Paul who could face the future without flinching. He said to his friends, ". . . What mean ye to weep and to break mine heart? for I am ready not to be bound only, but also to die at Jerusalem for the name of the Lord Jesus" (Acts 21:13). Many of us would like to come to that place of total commitment to Him.

Now notice that all things are working together for good for them "who are the called" ones, and it is "according to his purpose." This is something that is hard for a great many people to swallow. "The called" are those who not only have received an invitation, they have accepted it. And they were born from above. They know experientially the love of God. Paul describes three groups of people, and I think they are the three groups that are in the world today: "But we preach Christ crucified, unto the Jews a stumblingblock, and unto the Greeks foolishness: but unto them which are called, both Jews and Greeks, Christ the power of God, and the wisdom of God" (1 Cor. 1:23–24). (1) The Jews trusted in religion, rite and ritual. To them the Cross was a stumblingblock. (2) The Greeks (the Gentiles) trusted in philosophy and human wisdom. To them the Cross was foolishness. (3) "The called" were a group out of both Jews and Greeks who were chosen not because of their religion or wisdom. God called them. To them the Cross was the *dynamite* of God unto salvation. "The called" heard God's call. That is important.

Let me go back to my illustration of the turtles. Suppose you go down to a swamp, and there are ten turtles. You say to the turtles, "I'd like to teach you to fly." Nine of them say, "We're not interested. We like it down here; we feel comfortable in this environment." One turtle says, "Yes, I'd like to fly." *That* is the one which is called, and that is the one which is taught to fly. Now that doesn't have anything in the world to do with the other turtles. They are turtles because they are turtles. My friend, the lost are *lost* because they want it that way. There is not a person on topside of this world that is being forced to be lost. They are lost because they have chosen to be lost.

A boy down in my southland years ago wanted to join a church. So the deacons were examining him. They asked, "How did you get saved?" His answer was, "God did His part, and I did my part." They thought there was something wrong with his doctrine, so they questioned further. "What was God's part and what was your part?" His explanation was a good one. He said, "God's part was the saving, and my part was the sinning. I done run from Him as fast as my sinful heart and rebellious legs could take me. He done took out after me till he run me down." My friend, that is the way I got saved also.

This does not destroy or disturb the fact that "whosoever will may come" and "whosoever believeth." Henry Ward Beecher quaintly put it, "The elect are the whosoever wills and the non-elect are the whosoever won'ts." And it is all according to His purpose. And, my friend, if you have not yet got your mind reconciled to God's purpose and to God's will, it is time you are doing that, because this is His universe. He made it. I don't know why He made a round earth instead of a square one—He didn't ask me how I wanted it—He made it round because He wanted it round. My friend, His purpose is going to be carried out, and He has the wisdom and the power to carry it out. Whatever God does is right. Don't you criticize God and say He has no right to save whoever wants to be saved. He has the right to do it. He is just and He is loving, and anything my God does is right.

There was a great theologian in the past by the name of Simeon. In his sermons on Romans 8 he said there were three reasons why he preached on the doctrine of election: It laid the axe at the root of pride, presumption, and despair. I like that. My friend, there is no place for human pride in the doctrine of election. It is God's work, His wisdom, and His purpose that is being carried out. The will of God comes down out of eternity past like a great steamroller. Don't think you can stop it. In fact, you had better get on and ride.

For whom he did foreknow, he also did predestinate to be conformed to the image of his Son, that he might be the firstborn among many brethren.

Moreover whom he did predestinate, them he also called: and whom he called, them he also justified: and whom he justified, them he also glorified [Rom. 8:29–30].

"For" refers back to verse 28 to remind us that he is not talking about anybody being elected to be *lost*, but he is speaking of "the called," the predestined ones. Predestination never has any reference to the lost. You will never find it used in connection with them. If you ever hear someone talk about being predestined to be lost, you know he is not being scriptural.

Predestination means that, when God saves you, He is going to see you through. Whom He foreknew, He predestinated, and whom He predestinated, He called, and whom He called, He justified, and whom He justified, He glorified. In other words, this amazing section is on *sanctification*—yet, Paul does not even mention being sanctified. Why? Because sanctification is the work of God in the heart and life of the believer. This is God's eternal purpose. It just simply means this: When the Lord—who is the Great Shepherd of the Sheep, the Good Shepherd of the Sheep, and Chief Shepherd of the Sheep—starts out with one hundred sheep, He's going to come home with one hundred sheep; He will not lose one of them. You may remember that our Lord gave a parable about this, recorded in Luke 15. There was a shepherd, a good shepherd, who represents the Lord Jesus. One little old sheep got lost, got away. You would think He might say, "Well, let him go. We've got ninety-nine of them safe in the fold. That's a good percentage." Anyone raising sheep knows that if you get to market with a little over fifty percent of those that are born, you're doing well. But this is an unusual shepherd. He is not satisfied with ninety-nine. If He justifies one hundred sheep, He's going to glorify one hundred sheep. I'll make this rather personal. Someday He will be counting them in— "One, two, three, four, five . . . ninety-seven, ninety-eight, ninety-nine—where in the world is Vernon McGee? Well, it looks like he didn't make it. We'll let him go because a great many people didn't think he was going to make it anyway." My friend, thank God He won't let him go. That Shepherd is going after him. The doctrine of election means that the Lord will be coming home with *one hundred* sheep! This is not a frightful doctrine; it is a wonderful doctrine. It means that Vernon McGee's going to be there; and it means you are going to be there, my friend, if you have trusted Christ. This is a most comforting doctrine in these uncertain days in which we live.

**What shall we then say to these things? If God be for us, who can be against us? [Rom. 8:31].**

"What shall we then say to these things?" My answer is, "What can I say? This is so wonderful I have nothing to add!"

"Who can be against us?" God is on our side. Nobody will be able to bring a charge against us in His presence.

**He that spared not his own Son, but delivered him up for us all, how shall he not with him also freely give us all things? [Rom. 8:32].**

How wonderful that is! He did not spare His Son. He spared Abraham's son, but not His own. Since He gave His Son to die for us, He will give us all things that we need. Somebody may say, "But I may not be able to hold out." He is going to do that for you—He will *hold you.* His sheep are safe, my friend. It is not because they are smart sheep. A rancher in San Angelo, Texas, who raises sheep, told me, "Sheep are stupid!" Also they are defenseless. They don't have sharp claws or fangs to protect themselves. They can't even run very fast. They are little old helpless animals. If a little old sheep stands up and sings, "Safe am I," is that sheep safe? Yes. Smart sheep? No, stupid. That little sheep is safe because he has a wonderful Shepherd.

"How shall he not with him also freely give us all things?" Dwight L. Moody illustrated it somewhat like this: Suppose I go into the finest jewelry store in the land, and they bring out the loveliest diamond, and the owner says, "It's yours!" And I say, "You don't mean that you are giving me this valuable diamond!" He says, "Yes. I am giving it to you." If he gave it to me, do you think I would hesitate asking him for a piece of brown wrapping paper to wrap it up and take it home with me? My friend, since God gave his Son to die for you, don't you know that He is going to give you everything that is necessary in this life and in the life to come?

> Who shall lay any thing to the charge of God's elect? It is God that justifieth.
>
> Who is he that condemneth? It is Christ that died, yea rather, that is risen again, who is even at the right hand of God, who also maketh intercession for us [Rom. 8:33–34].

God's elect are justified sinners. God has placed His throne behind them. Who is going to condemn them? Nobody can condemn them. Why? "It is Christ that died, yea rather, that is risen again."

Christ has removed all condemnation, and the believer is secure because of the fourfold work of Christ: (1) Christ died for us—He was delivered for our offenses; (2) Christ was raised from the dead, raised for our justification; (3) He is on the right hand of God. He is up there right now, my friend. He is the living Christ. Do you need Him? Why don't you appeal to Him? (4) He maketh intercession for us. Did you pray for yourself this morning? You should have. But if you missed praying, He didn't. He prayed for you. How wonderful! This fourfold work of Christ is the reason that nobody can lay anything to the charge of God's elect.

> Who shall separate us from the love of Christ? shall tribulation, or distress, or persecution, or famine, or nakedness, or peril, or sword? [Rom. 8:35].

He mentions everything imaginable here.

Is it possible that "tribulation" or trouble can separate us? No, my friend, because He won't let it. "Distress or anguish?" Oh, you may think God has let you down, but He hasn't. "Persecution"—and this means legal persecution. It means there are those who will carry on a campaign against you. But that will not separate you from the love of Christ. "Or famine, or nakedness, or peril, or sword?" By the way, this is a brief biography of Paul's life. He knows from experience that those will not separate you from Christ's love.

> As it is written, For thy sake we are killed all the day long; we are accounted as sheep for the slaughter [Rom. 8:36].

This is a quotation from Psalm 44:22: ". . . yea, for thy sake are we killed all the day long; we are counted as sheep for the slaughter." This is a frightful picture of the saints in this day of grace. I believe with all my heart that this is the attitude of a satanic system toward the child of God even in this hour. Also the history of the church reveals this. My friend, if you stand for God today, it will cost you something.

My first job, as a kid about fifteen years old, was in an abatoir, a slaughterhouse. I worked right next to the man who took a sharp knife and cut the sheep's throat. To see animals slaughtered by the hundreds was a frightful spectacle. I got so sick I had to go outside and sit in the fresh air.

And, friend, it is sickening to see what is happening to some of the saints of God in our day. But even this will not separate us from the love of God.

> Nay, in all these things we are more than conquerors through him that loved us [Rom. 8:37].

How can a sheep for the slaughter be more than a conqueror? This is another wonderful paradox of the Christian faith. What does it mean to be more than a conqueror? It means to have assistance from another who gets the victory for us, who never lets us be defeated. The victory belongs to Christ; not to us. The victorious life is not our life. It is His life.

> **For I am persuaded, that neither death, nor life, nor angels, nor principalities, nor powers, nor things present, nor things to come,**
>
> **Nor height, nor depth, nor any other creature, shall be able to separate us from the love of God, which is in Christ Jesus our Lord [Rom. 8:38–39].**

"For I am persuaded" means that he *knows*.

"Death" cannot separate us—in fact, it will take us into His presence. The response of many of the early Christian martyrs when they were threatened with death was, "Thank you, you will transport me right into the presence of my Savior." You can't hurt people like that.

"Life"—often it is more difficult to face life than to face death. But life's temptations, failures, disappointments, uncertainties, and sufferings will not separate us from the love of God that is in Christ our Lord.

"Angels"—and I think he means fallen angels—"principalities and powers" are spiritual enemies of the believer (see Eph. 6:12).

"Things present" means present circumstances.

"Things to come" refers to the future.

"Nor height, nor depth" may refer to the space age in which we live.

"Any other created thing" would include anything else you want to mention. Absolutely nothing can separate us from the love of God which is centered in Christ.

My friend, salvation is a love story. We love Him because He first loved us. Nothing can separate us from that. We entered this chapter with no condemnation; we conclude it with no separation; and in between all things work together for good. Can you improve on this, friend? This is wonderful!

# BIBLIOGRAPHY
## (Recommended for Further Study)

Barnhouse, Donald Grey. *Romans*. 4 vols. Grand Rapids, Michigan: Wm. B. Eerdmans Publishing Co., 1952–1960. (Expositions of Bible doctrines, taking the Epistle to the Romans as a point of departure.)

DoHaan, Riohard W. *The World on Trial. Studies in Romans.* Grand Rapids, Michigan: Zondervan Publishing House, 1970.

Epp, Theodore H. *How God Makes Bad Men Good: Studies in Romans*. Lincoln, Nebraska: Back to the Bible Broadcast, 1978.

Hendriksen, William. *The Epistle to the Romans*. Grand Rapids, Michigan: Baker Book House, 1980.

Hodge, Charles. *Commentary on the Epistle to the Romans*. Grand Rapids, Michigan: Wm. B. Eerdmans Publishing Co., 1886.

Hoyt, Herman A. *The First Christian Theology: Studies in Romans*. Grand Rapids, Michigan: Baker Book House, 1977. (Good for group study.)

Ironside, H. A. *Lectures on Romans*. Neptune, New Jersey: Loizeaux Brothers, n.d. (Especially fine for young Christians.)

Jensen, Irving R. *Romans: Self-Study Guide*. Chicago, Illinois: Moody Press, n.d.

Johnson, Alan F. *Romans: The Freedom Letter*. Chicago, Illinois: Moody Press, 1974.

Kelly, William. *Notes on Romans*. Addison, Illinois: Bible Truth Publishers, 1873.

Luther, Martin. *Commentary on Romans*. 1516 Reprint. Grand Rapids, Michigan: Kregel Publications, 1976.

McClain, Alva J. *Romans: The Gospel of God's Grace*. Chicago, Illinois: Moody Press, 1942.

McGee, J. Vernon. *Reasoning Through Romans*. 2 vols. Pasadena, California: Thru the Bible Books, 1959.

Moule, Handley C. G. *The Epistle to the Romans*. Fort Washington, Pennsylvania: Christian Literature Crusade, n.d. (See note below.)

Moule, Handley C. G. *Studies in Romans*. Grand Rapids, Michigan: Kregel Publications, 1892. (Originally appeared in the Cambridge Bible for Schools and Colleges. These two books by Moule complement each other and are both excellent.)

Murray, John. *Romans*. Grand Rapids, Michigan: Wm. B. Eerdmans Publishing Co., 1965. (For advanced students.)

Newell, William R. *Romans Verse by Verse*. Chicago, Illinois: Moody Press, 1938. (An excellent study.)

Philips, John. *Exploring Romans*. Chicago, Illinois: Moody Press, 1969.

Stifler, James. *The Epistle to the Romans*. Chicago, Illinois: Moody Press, 1897.

Thomas, W. H. Griffith. *The Book of Romans*. Grand Rapids, Michigan: Wm. B. Eerdmans Publishing Co., 1946. (Fine interpretation.)

Vine, W. E. *Romans*. Grand Rapids, Michigan: Zondervan Publishing House, 1950.

Wuest, Kenneth S. *Romans in the Greek New Testament for English Readers*. Grand Rapids, Michigan: Wm. B. Eerdmans Publishing Co., 1955.

Wiersbe, Warren W. *Be Right. (Romans)*. Wheaton, Illinois: Victor Books, 1977.